HINDUJAS
and
BOLLYWOOD

AJIT RAI

TRANSLATED BY
MURTAZA ALI KHAN

Vani Book Company
An imprint of Vani Prakashan Group

Vani Book Company
(An Imprint of Vani Prakashan Group)
Head Office

4695, 21-A, Daryaganj, New Delhi 110 002, India
Phone : +91 11 23273167 Fax : +91 11 23275710

Registered Bookstores and Offices
Ashok Rajpath, Patna 800 004, Bihar
Coffee House Campus, Mahatma Gandhi Marg, Allahabad 211 001, Uttar Pradesh
Mahatma Gandhi International Hindi University, Wardha 442 001, Maharashtra
Goripur Taliya Para, 313, R.B.C. Road 24- Parganas (North) Kolkata 743 166, West Bengal

www.vaniprakashan.com
marketing@vaniprakashan.in
sales@vaniprakashan.in

Hindujas and Bollywood
Translated from the Hindi original
Bollywood Ki Buniyaad
by Ajit Rai
Translated by Murtaza Ali Khan

ISBN : 978-93-5518-077-3
History/Cinema

First Edition June 2022
Second Edition August 2022

Price : ₹ 595
$ 11
£ 8

Printed and bound in India at R. Tek offset Printers, Delhi-110032
Vani Prakashan's signature motif is created by Artist Maqbool Fida Husain

This Book is Dedicated to

Hinduja Brothers - *Shrichand, Gopichand, Prakash* and
Ashok Hinduja whose Blessings are my Capital

&

My Mother Smt. *Chinta Devi Rai* (Late) & Father
Shri *Bhola Nath Rai*, Village + P. O. Kasian, Dumraon,
Buxar Bihar, India

&

My dear Son *Bhargav Rai* who is a great lover
of Indian Cinema

&

All my friends who love Indian Cinema
and appreciate my writings

Acknowledgment

After having written over five thousand articles, reports, interviews, reviews, etc. in various newspapers and magazines, when destiny chose me to write this book, I kept remembering the following words of my friend Pankaj Narayan—"Just like talent is in need of an opportunity, opportunity too seeks talent". My meeting with Prakash Hinduja at the Cannes Film Festival, attending the Hinduja brothers' dinner at Villa Paradise, hearing 50s film stories from Gopichand Hinduja, Ashish Ahuja's phone call from Mumbai, meeting Gopichand ji in London, and planning to write a book like this—it was all just sheer coincidence. Owing to the COVID-19 pandemic and partly due to my lazy nature, it took me two extra years to write this book.

Many people have contributed directly or indirectly in the making of this book. The biggest contribution of course is that of the Hinduja brothers—Gopichand ji, Prakash ji and Ashok Hinduja ji. They always made themselves available on the phone despite their busy schedules. Also, I will forever be grateful to Ashish Ahuja, Vice President - Corporate Communications, Hinduja Group (Mumbai) for his constant support and suggestions. I am grateful to Murli Chhabria, Ramesh Nichani, Sanjay Jumani, Subhash Sharma, Sanjay Khan, Dharmendra, Amit Khanna, Prem Sagar, Ketan Desai, Anu Malik, S.M. Khan, senior BBC journalist Rehan Fazal and all those who took time out of their busy schedule to talk to me on this topic. Mumbai-based Abin Das and Gulnar Maroliya, personal secretary of Prakash Hinduja, assisted me in connecting to many people. Also, I would like to extend my gratitude to Raj Kapoor's daughter Ritu Nanda whose book 'Raj Kapoor: The One and Only Showman' proved to be very helpful. I would also like to thank Ram Kripal Singh, Executive Editor of 'Navbharat Times,' and Sundar Chandra Thakur, Editor of the Mumbai Edition of 'Navbharat Times,' for sending me to the Cannes Film Festival (2013) as the representative on behalf of the 'Times of India Publications Group'. I would like to extend my gratitude to the professors at Mumbai University, Mangesh Bansod (Theatre), Sundar Rajdeep (Journalism), and Karuna Shankar Upadhyay (Hindi) for always wholeheartedly welcoming me to Mumbai. I cannot forget India's famous actor Ajay Kumar who kept me with him at Mukul Anand's flat during my stay in Mumbai and took care of each and everything. Thanks to Anuj Garg who took me with him to the Cannes Film Festival (2013) for the first time.

The publishing of this book would have given the greatest pleasure to my elder brother Tejendra Sharma who has always guided me and hosted me at his house for months on end several times in London. I am blessed to have a mentor like senior journalist Girija Shankar ji from Bhopal who helped remove obstacles from my path and who has been a constant source of encouragement.

I cannot miss out on mentioning Mumbai's Dharmendra Nath Ojha and Akshat Pandey who are a beacon of positive energy. Both of them always motivated me to complete this book as quickly as possible.

The blessings of Shri Achyutanand Mishra and Shri Devendra Raj Ankur, who are my gurus in journalism and theatre, have always been with me. I am grateful to my editors who trusted me and gave space to my writings, including Mukesh Bhardwaj (Jansatta), Laxmi Prasad Pant (Dainik Bhaskar), Dilip Choubey (National Sahara), Subhash Rai (Jansandesh Times), Pankaj Shukla (Amar Ujala), Subhash Mishra (Aaj Ki Jandhara), Rajiv Agnihotri (People's News), Chandra Bhushan (Navbharat Times), and Prakash K Ray (Prabhat Khabar), among others. I am also grateful to the dozens of digital media platforms which have published my articles.

The famous French actress Marianne Borgo who lives in Paris and the Labor Party counselor in London, Zakia Zubairi, have adopted me in a way. After the death of my own mother Mrs. Chinta Devi Rai (15 July, 2020), having these godmothers in my life is nothing less than a boon. While writing this book, I got the support of many friends from abroad to whom I am very grateful. Here I would especially like to mention my German journalist friend Alice Kanterian, with whom I have always stayed at Cannes during the Film Festival for the last ten years.

I am falling short of words to express my gratitude to the publisher of the book Vani Prakashan's Arun Maheshwari, with whom I have been friends for the last 30 years, and his gifted and enterprising daughter Aditi Maheshwari-Goyal.

In the end, I am grateful to my mother Mrs. Chinta Devi Rai (Late), and father Mr. Bhola Nath Rai whose blessings are my strength. I am also grateful to my two sisters—Seema and Neebha—and four brothers—Bablu, Mintu, Rinku and Dinesh Kumar—who have stood by me through thick and thin.

Ajit Rai
Email: ajitraieditor@gmail.com

New Delhi
15 June, 2022

Translator's Note

It was when Ajit Rai invited me to the Azamgarh International Film Festival a few years back that I truly began to appreciate his endearing love for India and Indian cinema. As the director of the festival, he hasn't left any stone unturned in making the festival a nurturing hub for film lovers in a rather remote part of the Indian hinterland. And, it is with the same love that he brings to light in his groundbreaking book, 'Hindujas and Bollywood,' the untold story of the global journey of over 1200 Hindi films as undertaken by the Hinduja brothers, starting with the 1950s.

In my decade and a half long career as a film journalist, I have seldom read something as riveting, compelling, and eye-opening written about Indian cinema. And, it is nothing less than a masterclass in film history. To have learnt that Raj Kapoor was the biggest global movie icon of the '60s and that the Hinduja brothers played an important role in it. That his popularity in Iran, Russia, and many other countries across the world surpassed the popularity of Presidents & Heads of States. And that he once had to be carried away in a prison car after the premiere of his film in Tehran in order to guard him from his overzealous fans who were dying for his one glimpse. That his 1964 blockbuster film 'Sangam' ran housefull for 3 years in Iran. That, in the able hands of the Hindujas brothers, the Hindi cinema totally outclassed and overshadowed Hollywood in Iran as well as the whole of Middle East. That the Hindujas made Bollywood a huge brand in not just Iran but also in the UK as well as Egypt, Turkey, Beirut, Greece, Israel, Thailand, etc.

With Ajit Rai' s lucid yet evocative language, borne out of decades of experience covering films, the sprawling narrative unfolds like an unforgettable saga oozing with cinematic splendor worthy of the story of the origins of Bollywood. It is also the story of the ubiquitous popularity of Hindi classics like 'Awaara,' 'Sholay,' 'Guide,' 'Sangam,' etc. There are whirlwind adventures galore as well as deeply personal accounts of immortal superstars and what made them human in spite of their fortunes and fame.

And, so, on undertaking the task of translating Ajit Rai's ground breaking work about the Hinduja brothers' role in establishing Bollywood as a global brand, I was overcome by a sense of thrill and dread, in equal parts. Thrill, because I had been chosen to play a small part in the retelling of a monumental journey which laid the foundations of Bollywood. Dread, because I could feel the burden of history over my shoulders.

Today, Bollywood is widely recognised as a global brand and it's almost synonymous with India in the global arena. But, not many people will believe me if today I told them that around seven decades ago, the Hinduja brothers started this global journey of Hindi films long before the moniker 'Bollywood' got attached to the Hindi film industry. That they helped produce countless films long before NFDC came into being and long before banks started lending money to the film producers.

While translating Ajit ji's monumental work of cinema history into English, I came to terms with the passion and commitment of the Hinduja brothers for India, its culture and its people, and the humanity at large as perfectly captured by their Gandhian father Parmanand Deepchand Hinduja's mantra, 'Work to Give.'

This is not just the story of the global journey of over 1200 Hindi films; this is also the story of the origins of the global brand of Hindi cinema that the whole world today refers to as Bollywood. This is also the story of Ajit Rai's quest to bring this fascinating, hitherto untold story to light which first began to take form during the 2017 Cannes Film Festival when Ajit Rai was first introduced to Gopichand Hinduja by his younger brother Prakash Hinduja at the Hinduja brothers' annual vegetarian dinner at their Cannes abode, Villa Paradise. On hearing Gopichand Hinduja talk about the deep association of the Hinduja brothers with Hindi cinema starting with the '50s, Ajit Rai solemnly pledged to bring this untold story to life in the form of a book. And the rest, as they say, is history!

Lastly and most importantly, this is also a tribute to Late Parmanad Deepchand Hinduja, who, driven by the principles of trade learnt from the 5000 year old Indus Valley Civilization, left the city of Shikarpur in the Sind Province (now in Pakistan) of Undivided India to pursue business opportunities in Bombay at the young age of 13 in the year 1914, and his children, Late Girdhar Hinduja, Srichand Hinduja, Gopichand Hinduja, Prakash Hinduja and Ashok Hinduja, who not only took their father's business from Iran to many other parts of the world, making it truly global, but also dedicated themselves to spreading Indian culture and values far and wide by taking these 1200 odds Hindi films to the Middle East, Far East as well as Europe.

A major challenge for me was to be true to Ajit Rai's exhaustively researched original text, both in letter and in spirit. And, so, it was most important to regularly consult him in these matters. Therefore, I had to be constantly in touch with him, whether on call, email, or WhatsApp. I am grateful to him for making himself available round the clock even when we were working in different timelines and despite his very busy schedule, especially while covering the 75th Cannes Film Festival in May, 2022.

Therefore, I would like to extend my deepest gratitude to Ajit Rai for trusting me with the responsibility to translate such as important and scholarly work of cinema history into the English language.

Murtaza Ali Khan

Email : murtaza.jmi@gmail.com

Contents

1

Hinduja Brothers' Vegetarian Dinner at the Cannes Film Festival and a Global Tour of 1200 Hindi Films

And this is how the plan to write the book was hatched

Every year Cannes Film Festival remains incomplete for me until I get to meet and chat with Gopichand Parmanand Hinduja and Prakash Parmanand Hinduja, the Indian-born richest citizens of Britain, there. Only two dinners are the talk of the town during the Cannes Film Festival—the opening dinner hosted by the Festival Director Thierry Frémaux at Majestic Beach and the vegetarian Indian cuisine reception at Villa Paradise, hosted by UK's richest Indian industrialists, the Hinduja brothers, wherein I met them for the first time on the evening of 20 May, 2017. They have been organizing this dinner since time immemorial and celebrities from every region of India and France have been attending it. Dev Anand himself attended the banquet when his film 'Guide' had a special screening at Cannes. Dev Anand himself told this to me when we happened to meet in Goa. Gopichand Parmanand Hinduja's humility and his act of giving respect to the other person touched my heart. While shaking hands with him, it feels as if something Great is about to happen.

There is an interesting anecdote about the beginning of this friendship over cinema. It is also interesting to learn how from Raj Kapoor's film 'Shree 420' (1954) to Amitabh Bachchan's 'Coolie' and 'Naseeb,' the global journey of about 1200 Hindi films (1954 -1984) was made possible by the Hinduja brothers. And this is how our Bollywood industry got established. His ambition still is that Indian films should rule the whole world and one day beat Hollywood. Even his brother Prakash P Hinduja is a singularly wonderful man. He is a walking-talking encyclopedia of cinema.

I remember it was in May 2016 when the responsibility of setting up and running the Indian Pavilion at the world's largest and most prestigious film festival, the Cannes Film Festival, was assigned to the Federation of Indian Chambers of Commerce and Industry (FICCI) by the Ministry of Information and Broadcasting, Government of India. Earlier this task was taken care of by the National Film Development Corporation (NFDC), under the leadership of Vikramjit Rai. Leena Jaisani, Director and Head, Media and Entertainment, FICCI, has been performing this responsibility brilliantly. She used to read my

Kamal Prakash Hinduja, Sharmila Tagore and Prakash Hinduja

daily reports in Indian newspapers from the Cannes Film Festival. It was here during an event that I met the famous media personality, Uday Shankar. I knew that just like me, he too comes from Bihar. Most of the serious film critics of my nature who come to the Cannes Film Festival focus mainly on the films in the Official Selection. So we often miss out on the news about the other activities. Later on, Mukesh Bhardwaj, editor of Jansatta, and Sundar Chandra Thakur, editor of Navbharat Times (Mumbai) made a suggestion that I should also include the Indian activities at the Cannes Film Festival in my report. One day, Leena Jaisani requested me to write a report on the activities of the Indian Pavilion. I obliged her and my report appeared in many Indian newspapers on 22 May, 2016. The title of that report was 'Indian Dreams in World Cinema'. Along with it, a photo featuring Rajyavardhan Singh Rathod, then Minister of State for Information and Broadcasting, FICCI President (Media and Entertainment) Uday Shankar, senior filmmaker Sudhir Mishra, India's Ambassador to France Mohan Kumar, and other concerned persons releasing the poster for the 47th International Film Festival of India (IFFI) to be held in Goa that year was also published. That was the beginning of a good friendship with Leena Jaisani.

Sanjay Jumani, A. R. Rahman and Prakash Hinduja

A year later, in May 2017, for some reason, Leena Jaisani could not come to the Cannes Film Festival. I was told that she was not well. I too could not go to the Indian Pavilion due to my busy schedule. On the afternoon of 19 May, 2017, I was able to finish my work of writing new reports a bit early and so I thought of paying a visit to the Indian Pavilion. All Indian journalists and people associated with cinema often visit the Indian Pavilion for internet and for tea. There is also a networking cocktail in the evening, wherein liquor is served along with samosas as well as some delicious Indian savouries. As soon as I reached the Indian Pavilion that day, Leena Jaisani's assistant told me in a complaining tone that perhaps I had forgotten the way to the Indian Pavilion. She then passed on a message from Leena Jaisani requesting me to attend the 'Sellers Buyers Meet' of the Indian and European filmmakers organized by FICCI on the first floor of the JW Marriott Hotel, and, if possible, during the lunchtime. FICCI organizes an annual festival on the entertainment industry in Mumbai called FICCI Frames every year. That event was organized under the banner of FICCI Frames 2018 which was to be held next year.

It was 2:30 in the afternoon and I started walking towards the JW Marriott Hotel. Little did I know that a life defining event awaited me there. The design of the stairs, which were made to go from the lobby of JW Marriott Hotel to the first floor, was such that they went up from the floor on two sides and met in the middle. From there the stairs went up on both sides in opposite directions and reached the first floor. I was walking up the stairs humming some song. As soon as I reached the middle of the staircase, an Indian gentleman in Bermuda shorts and T-shirt and wearing a cap was descending from the first floor. He had some papers in his hand. He was accompanied by another Indian, who may have been his assistant. Now we were face to face in the middle of the staircase. He recognized me by my dress and mannerism that I too wasan Indian. I was wearing black jeans and a long black kurta and as per my habit, a colored gamcha was wrapped around my neck. He cheerfully asked me on seeing me—"How are you?"

Waving my gamcha, I said, "Paramanand Hai (I feel blissful)!"

I did not know until then that Parmanand was his father's name, Shri Parmanand Deepchand Hinduja (1901–1971).

He further asked, "And how is the Cannes Film Festival going?"

I said, "Great."

He asked, "Which all movies are good?"

I said, "There are many. Bong Joon Ho's 'Okja' (South Korea), Andrey Zvyagintsev's 'Loveless' (Russia), Naomi Kawase's 'Hikari' (Japan), Fateh Akin's 'In the Fade' (Germany), Michael Haneke's 'Happy End' (Austria), Ruben Ostlund's 'The Square' (Sweden), Michel Hazanavicius' 'Redoutable' (France), Roman Polanski's 'Based on a True Story' are some of the movies that are a must watch.

As per my habit, I spoke fluently. He kept listening. After I had finished, he said with great affection, "Tomorrow on May 20, at eight o'clock in the evening, some guests are coming to my house for dinner, you also please come." He asked his assistant to write my name and phone number on the guest list. His assistant handed me an invitation card.

"Where do you live?" he asked

I said, "Delhi. And you?"

Showing the Cannes Film Festival badge hanging around his neck, he said, "I live in the whole world. Come home the day after tomorrow. Then we will talk." I took his badge near my eyes and saw it. It read Prakash P Hinduja. Before I could thank him for the dinner invitation, he had already left with his assistant. So, I went upstairs where I met Bobby Bedi.

From there I came back to the 'Palais des Festivals' (the building where the Cannes Film Festival takes place, that is, the main venue of the festival). The Cannes Film Festival on its 70th anniversary opened a luxurious Media Lounge for film critics on the fourth floor of the 'Palais des Festivals' where we could relax while watching a panoramic view of the blue sea and eat and drink while contemplating about the films, press conferences and our reports to be written. Here, beer, wine, juice, soft drinks, etc., along with light snacks are always available for journalists, and that too absolutely free of cost. This happens to be my favourite place during the Cannes Film Festival. There is also a media lounge on the third floor, which is run by the telecom company Orange, but only tea-coffee, water-juice, soda, etc. are served there. On the second floor below, the telecom company HP operates a huge media hall but nothing is available there except water. But there are hundreds of well-equipped computers to work there. In the other two media lounges, we have to work on our own devices.

On carefully reading the invitation card given by Prakash P Hinduja's assistant, I was shocked. It was clearly written—Hinduja Parivar, the Hinduja Group and Extravagant India—International Indian Film Festival, Paris—feels delighted to invite you to celebrate India's Independence and the Seventieth Anniversary of Cannes Film Festival with Indian Vegetarian Cuisine on Saturday, 20th May 2017 evening 8 to 10 o'clock. The address given was—Villa Paradisiaque (meaning Villa Paradise), 22 Avenue, Sol Mio, 06400, Cannes. Also, there was an instruction to RSVP by the morning of Friday, May 19th. Alice Kantarian had explained to me two years ago that for all the invites that come during the Cannes Film Festival, one has to RSVP as only then one can get admission there. But what could have I done? I had received the invitation only on the afternoon of May

Prakash Hinduja with the artists from the Middle East during the Cannes Film Festival

19. I checked the location of the Hinduja brothers' villa on Google. I found out that there was no connecting bus or tram to that place. In order to reach there, I would have to take a taxi whose fare would be at least two and a half thousand Indian rupees. The two-way trip to the Hinduja dinner and back would cost me five thousand Indian rupees. I calculated that for five thousand Indian rupees, I could have a great dinner at least five times in any restaurant in Cannes. Please don't get me wrong, I am not a stingy person! But every Indian who comes to the Cannes Film Festival tries to save every penny because it is a very expensive place. So I decided that I would not go to the dinner party of the Hinduja brothers. And the matter was quickly forgotten as I got busy with my work.

My routine during the Cannes Film Festival is very hectic and tiring. One has to get up early in the morning at 6:30 and get ready. The essential items are packed in the bag before sleeping every night. The first show at the Grand Theatre Lumiere is at 8:30 in the morning, which is for the press only. This is the premiere show of all the films in the competition section of the Cannes Film

Festival. For this, we have to reach at eight o'clock in the morning and have to stand in line or else they close all the doors. I have a priority, and in one way, a VIP press card so this line is shorter for me. You can't go inside once the show starts. The show ends at half past ten or quarter to eleven and the press conference of that film takes place at eleven o'clock. By 12.30 pm, I come to the media lounge on the fourth floor and start writing. After sending reports and photos to Indian newspapers by 2.30 pm, there is a little free time for an hour because at that time it is 6:30 pm in India and normally the deadline for the national news page is 7 o'clock. During this time, there is fun and frolicking with friends in the Indian pavilion as well as the pavilions of other countries. In this, my guide is my German journalist friend, Alice Kanterian, in whose apartment I have stayed since 2015. There is an entire story behind meeting Alice and making friends with her. Press shows at the Debussy Theater take place at 4 pm, 7 pm, and 10 pm. Then the round of night parties begins. After reaching my room and taking a bath, it is two o'clock at night. By then it is half past five in the morning in India and all the newspapers are already uploaded on the internet. One is so tired by then that one falls asleep while reading them. This routine remains for twelve days. Watching movies and writing about them.

There are about seven categories of press cards at the Cannes Film Festival. The press cards of the seven categories are of different colour. They are recognized by these colors and on this basis, there is a separate line to go for each activity. I was first authorized by the editor of Navbharat Times Mumbai, Sundar Chandra Thakur, for the press accreditation of the Cannes Film Festival in 2013 with a letter from the Times of India Newspaper Group and so the very first year itself I got the fifth grade press card from the bottom. It is pink in colour. The press card below it is colored blue and then yellow and orange. The lowest priority card is colored green. In fact, I was the first Hindi journalist to reach this point in the history of the Cannes Film Festival so far (1946-2013). It was a matter of pride and joy for me. In the same year, the very first year of my appearance at the Cannes Film Festival, my article titled 'Darwaze Par Hi Raha Atithi Desh (Guest Country Remained at the Door Only)' went viral. After reading this article, while doing 'Tattva Chintan' (drinking red wine) at Cafe Roma, the famous Parisian Indian filmmaker Vijay Singh said, "Ajit, you are the first Indian film critic to tell Indians what the Cannes

Film Festival is like after all. I will ask the press chief Christine Amy to felicitate you in her office. Your coming here is a big event for the Hindi society." That evening my friend Tripurari Sharan was also with me at Cafe Roma. In fact, the Cannes Film Festival had given India the status of a guest country that year, but not a single Indian film was in the official selection. I believe this was because France had won a huge contract for Rafale aircraft, overtaking the US. When I walked on the Red Carpet of the Cannes Film Festival for the first time on 19th May 2013 with my friend and my sponsor of that year, Anuj Garg, I had tears in my eyes. As a child, I used to get beaten up for my passion for cinema and the same passion had brought me to the Red Carpet of Cannes Film Festival, which is the world's biggest and most prestigious film festival.

Ajit Rai at the Hinduja brother's dinner party at Villa Paradise during the Cannes Film Festival

Three years later, impressed by my work at the 69th Cannes Film Festival held in 2016, on the recommendation of Christine Amy, Head of Press at the Cannes Film Festival, the festival upgraded my press card to a sixth grade called 'Pink with Yellow Dot'. This means that the Cannes Film Festival has included me in the list of the most important film critics of the world. Very few (about one hundred and fifty) journalists get this press card out of about five thousand journalists who come from all over the world to cover the Cannes Film Festival. Above this, there is only one category i.e. the seventh category which is called 'White'. In most places, there is only one line for these two categories. The White Press Card is awarded to journalists who have been reporting for the Cannes Film Festival for several decades and who work for the world's largest and most prestigious media groups. Till now no Indian journalist has got the White Press Card. Getting the high priority 'Pink with Yellow Dot' press card was more important for me because I had achieved this for doing reporting from the Cannes Film Festival in my mother tongue Hindi. The neglect and humiliation faced by journalists reporting in Hindi at the IFFI which is held every year in Goa is shameful and unjust. I remember when I went to Goa in 2006 to cover the festival for Jansatta, I was not even invited to the inauguration ceremony simply because they didn't think our newspaper was prestigious enough. I protested a lot in front of the officers of thePress Information Bureau. I even called my editor. He advised me to speak to Neelam Kapoor who was then the Director-General of PIB. On her orders, I got the invitation letter. Hindi film journalists are usually not included in any activity or on the jury of the Directorate of Film Festivals under the Ministry of Information and Broadcasting, Government of India. That's why the honor and respect accorded by the Cannes Film Festival to a Hindi journalist like me was totally unexpected.

I had almost forgotten about the Hinduja brothers' dinner. Next day i.e. on Saturday, 20th May, 2017, as soon as I wound up my writing work, I checked my email and found a mail from Gabriele Brennan of Paris, which was an invitation to the Hinduja brothers' dinner. This invitation had already been extended to me by the associate of Prakash P Hinduja the day before. Reading this again, I was struck by the fact that the event was being organized jointly by Gabriele Brennan's organization 'Extravagant India—International Indian Film Festival, Paris'. How could this happen? I was later told by Marianne Borgo that the man in Cannes who oversaw all the work of the Hinduja group had suddenly left the job. In such a case, Gabriele Brennan and her colleagues may have agreed to co-ordinate the event on the condition that the invitation card also bears her name and that of her organization and that they are given equal credit. I learned later that the Hinduja family has never been interested in taking credit. These people just believe in doing good things. So, naturally, they would have easily accepted Gabrielle Brennan's conditions. I already knew Gabrielle Brennan. She has been doing great work for Indian cinema in Paris in collaboration with Mumbai-based filmmaker Ramesh Tekwani. She rents a ship in the river outside Paris and organizes an event to encourage young French filmmakers wherein her films are screened and discussed. I have also been there with Marianne Borgo and Anjou Bala Probst. Suddenly, I received a call from Marianne Borgo. She asked me if I had received the invitation to the Hinduja brothers' dinner. I replied, "Yes." My first meeting with Marianne Borgo had been at the Indian Film Festival in Berlin's Babylon Cinema in August 2012 where Manoj Srivastava had sent me in his place as the Festival Director. I was trying to charm her actress friend of Italian descent named Kaia Bernert. Today, there is no trace of Kaia in my life but Marianne Borgo has been my friend, philosopher, and guide since 2014. I have stayed with her in Goa. In Paris also, I stay at her place only.But that is a different story for some other time. An idea immediately came to my mind. Since Marianne was anyway going to take a taxi to the Hinduja dinner, I thought of accompanying her, hoping to get dropped off midway on our way back from where I would walk back to my apartment. There was only one fear that she might tell me that she would be going there on her cycle. Actually, the bungalow where she was staying was four to five kilometers away from the main place of the festival and so she commuted to the festival every day from there on her cycle. She would rest her cycle on a pole anywhere on the roadside and would start walking because thefts there are very rare. But I felt that an elite woman like Marianne Borgo would not go to dinner at the villa of the Hinduja brothers on a bicycle. I asked Marianne if she was going to dinner and if I could accompany her in her car or taxi. She immediately said, "Of course," and gave the address of her bungalow—5 Rue du Golfe Juan. She also told me that the number eight Palm bus from the festival would drop him near her bungalow. I had no time to go to my room, take a shower and change, and go to Marianne Borgo's bungalow. I remembered my seniors' teaching that there is no dress code for journalists and reporters. I took the number eight bus and got down at the spot as per the instructions given by Marianne Borgo. I didn't have to wander much. On reaching, I saw that two women who had to go to the dinner were already present there.

When we reached the Hinduja brothers' Villa Paradise, we had to get down from the taxi at the main gate itself. At the main gate, the doorman bowed down and gave us a salute. Passing through a long lawn, we came to another main door where a man was checking the names of the invited guests and was letting them in only after ticking against their names on the list. When my turn came, he was confused as he could not find my name on the list. Suddenly a voice instructed him to let me in; probably it was Gabriele Brennan's. The man then politely said, "Please, welcome." When we enter Villa Paradise, the three-foot bronze statue of Ganesha on the right immediately captures our attention. Later on, I also saw a similar grand statue of Ganesha in the London house of the Hinduja brothers. After crossing a large verandah, I reached the party venue where about two hundred men and women were already gathered.People had gathered around a large lawn with a swimming pool in the middle. Some people were also there in the verandah upstairs. Prakash Hinduja gave me a warm welcome. He asked me, "Would you like to meet Gopi? Let me introduce you." I asked, "Who is Gopi?"

He said, "By Gopi, I mean my elder brother Gopichand Hinduja." I hurriedly said, "Yes, yes, I would love to meet him." He held my hand and took me to meet Gopichand Hinduja. Introducing me to him, he said, without hesitation, "This is Mr. Ajit Rai, India's greatest film journalist. He has come from Navbharat Times, Mumbai."

I and Gopichand Hinduja were now face to face. For a moment it felt as if time had stopped. We were looking at each other. He patted both my shoulders and said, "God bless you." Without wasting any time, I made him promise to meet me in London. He gave the phone number of his personal secretary, Sharmili. I was stunned to see that he remembers all the phone numbers by heart. Suddenly, he was called to the stage.

Bhuvan Lal was conducting the stage.

After the ceremonial reception, Gopichand Hinduja recounted how he had screened around twelve hundred Hindi films across the world, and no film ever suffered any loss. His ambition still is that Indian films should rule the whole world and one day beat Hollywood. He projected a roadmap for how Indian films can dominate the world market. He cited the worldwide success of Raj Kapoor's 'Sangam'. No one could have imagined in 1964 that a Hindi film would run for two weeks in London and make profit. In Iran and Egypt, the film ran in the theatres for three years. Gopichand Hinduja, who has screened about twelve hundred Hindi films, said if we can work together, we will be able to beat Hollywood. He said that it is unfortunate that every year thirteen hundred films are made in India and yet our participation in the world market of cinema is negligible. Even today only Satyajit Ray is known in France. Indian cinema after him did not get as much importance and market in France as it should have. He said that there is a need to revive the Indian potential in art cinema. French filmmakers should be involved more and more in Indian film production so that our art cinema can find a place in France.

I was listening to them in awe. How did our Bollywood come into being? How did Hindi films get global recognition? Today our films are doing good business all over the world. This became possible because about sixty-five years ago the Hinduja brothers started it all from Iran and gradually they took Hindi cinema to the whole world.The unwritten pages of the history of Indian cinema were opening before me which people generally do not know about. It was then that an idea came to my mind to write a book on the global and cultural journey of twelve hundred Hindi films. I had made up my mind to write the book.

A dinner party at the Hinduja brothers' residence at Villa Paradise during the Cannes Film Festival

I suddenly noticed that the party had turned colourful. I remember Gopichand Hinduja telling Jet Airways owner Naresh Goyal that there was no direct flight from India to visit the Cannes Film Festival and they should start at least one special flight from Mumbai to Nice during this festival. That's when I noticed that the Indian filmmaker settled in Paris Vijay Singh had arrived. From the midst of India's ambassador to France, Mohan Kumar, and a large number of people, Sanjay Jumani, a relative of the Hinduja brothers, took me aside to the counter where liquor was being served. It made me ecstatic. The Scotch counter was completely empty. Most people were drinking wine and beer. I just couldn't hold back any longer. I drank scotch nonstop and ate rice with lentils and brinjal curry fiercely. When I came to my senses, I discovered myself with Sanjay Jumani on the edge of the swimming poolin an inebriated state. It was twelve o'clock in the night and all the other guests had already left except the two of us. Then I saw Prakash Hinduja coming towards us.He felt that I was no longer in a condition to go alone. He asked Sanjay Jumani to drop me at my apartment in his car. In the middle of the night, Sanjay Jumani put me in his small, toy-like car, and off we went. Coming outside the main gate, he asked me for the address of my apartment. I was half asleep. I said with great difficulty, "163, Boulevard de la République." I was lucky that as soon as I got down the hill, I remembered my way. The paths on which you walk continuously, those paths recognize you. On reaching my room, I checked my news reports published in Indian newspapers as usual and typed 'Gopichand Hinduja' on Google. I was shocked to see what I saw. Google told me that Gopichand Hinduja, whom I had just met, happened to be the richest man in England. Till then I had only heard the name of the Hinduja brothers. I didn't know anything about their wealth. Then I remembered that the Hinduja brothers regularly get mentioned in India Today's list of most influential people. I was amazed by his simplicity and humility. I was determined that I would definitely write about this unwritten history of cinema.

HARÉ RAMA
HARÉ KRISHNA

JUGNU

2

Britain's Richest man
was traveling with me
on the Streets
of Mumbai in a
simple Auto Rickshaw

It was getting very hot that day in London. The heat had broken the record of the last forty years. The date was Wednesday 21 June 2017. It was the longest day of the year. After walking out of London's Trafalgar Square Underground (metro station), when I reached New Zealand House (80 Hay Market, London SW1 Y4TE), the office of the Hinduja Group, it was about quarter to five in the evening. My elder brother Tejendra Sharma had explained to me exactly how I could reach Trafalgar Square from Harrow and Wealdstone Railway Station. I was to meet Shri Gopichand Parmanand Hinduja, Co-Chairman of the Hinduja Group at five o'clock. I told my name to the receptionist and immediately a young man came out from that side and asked me to come with him. He dropped me by a special lift to the fourteenth floor. This lift did not stop at any floor in between. On reaching the top floor there was another reception. The receptionist there escorted me to the waiting room where I was served tea along with a sumptuous Indian breakfast. After a short while, I was taken to Gopichand Hinduja's room. When I touched his feet, he was very embarrassed and said—

"Oh no, my friend, please don't touch my feet. This is the UK, not India."

I said—"It may be the UK for you, but I feel very much like India here at your office and in your company."

After the formalities, our main conversation started for which I was there. I said—"What the Hinduja brothers have done for Indian cinema, our new generation does not know and the old generation has almost forgotten about it. It is necessary to write that golden history. People should know how Bollywood came to be. Today, our films are doing good business all over the world, but it was you guys who started it all about sixty-five years ago.

I also made it clear that I will write this book in Hindi. I continued to say—"There are many reasons behind this. First, I have earned so much respect and importance at the Cannes Film Festival by writing in Hindi. Also, Hindi is my mother tongue. The Prime Minister of India, the President, the Speaker of the Lok Sabha, and almost the entire cabinet read in Hindi. We are going to write about the global journey of Hindi cinema. Hindi is understood by most people of our country."

I said one more thing—"You also talk to your own people in Hindi and speak in English only while talking to your employees."

Amrita Singh with Srichand, Sanjay, Prakash, and Gopichand Hinduja in front of the Hinduja brothers' yacht Param Jamuna during the Cannes Film Festival

He asked his assistant to connect him to Ashish Ahuja in Mumbai. He turned on the speaker phone and started talking about my plan to write a book. It seemed to me that Ashish Ahuja was a bit unsure about Hindi. Gopichand Hinduja assured him that later he could get the book printed in other languages as well such as English, German and French. I recalled that after meeting Gopichand and Prakash Hinduja in Cannes, on Monday, 22 May, 2017, Ashish Ahuja had called me from Mumbai and introduced himself saying that he looked after Corporate Communications for Hinduja Group. He then assured me if I wanted any more information, I could take it from him. I also made it clear to Gopichand ji that I did not want any remuneration or honorarium from them for writing the book. I said—"Your blessings are my wealth."

Gopichand ji blessed me and said—"You have come on a very auspicious day. Today is the longest day of the year. Look, the sun is shining outside. The sun of the British has set. The brightness that we are seeing here, it is because of we Indians. God bless you." He gave me some gifts including a precious Parker pen which is my most prized possession.

Dev Anand with Srichand Hinduja at the Hinduja Brothers' dinner during the Cannes Film Festival

I took a bird's eye view of London from the fourteenth floor of New Zealand House. From here, London appeared to me as if it were under the feet of the Indians. The British Empire on which the sun never used to set, it will be one day be run by the Indians. The thought itself excited me. The 13-16, Carlton House Terrace where the Hinduja brothers live today in London was once the home of Britain's Queen Victoria. That evening in London with the richest man in England was very special. To meet Shri Gopichand Parmanand Hinduja and talk about Indian cinema was like going through a chapter of history that we had forgotten. He had agreed to my idea of writing the book. I wanted to ask him when he would be buying the Buckingham Palace of Queen Elizabeth II of

Britain. A year later, crossing the street between St James's Park and his house, I actually asked him, pointing to Buckingham Palace—"When are you buying this palace." He laughed and said—"You are very naughty." His youngest brother Ashok Hinduja is a witness to this incident.

Coming down from the fourteenth floor of the New Zealand house, I asked the receptionist for the address of the Brazilian embassy. Actually, one of my friends, Rakesh K Mathur, had invited me that evening to a colorful program organized at the Embassy of Brazil. While extending the invitation, he had said—"Have a lot of fun."Vinod Bhardwaj, the eminent cultural journalist, had told me a lot from time to time about the interesting life of Rakesh Mathur. At one point, Rakesh Mathur had worked for the famous film magazine 'Madhuri' of the Times of India Group published from Mumbai. He has been deeply associated with the cultural activities of London. It was also Rakesh Mathur who had introduced me to mainstream cultural activities in London. I don't know why but I have always been attracted to Brazilian women. I also love Brazilian cinema. I will write about that evening and night some other time. Gopichand ji had come till the lift to drop me. From there, one of his assistants came down to drop me. I thanked them both. I was very happy. But there is a story behind this meeting as well.

Gopichand Hinduja at the Cannes Film Festival

It has been happening for the past few years that on the second or third day after the conclusion of the Cannes Film Festival, Marianne Borgo and I would catch a superfast train at 5:27 pm from the Cannes railway station to Paris. I would sleep for two or three days at Marianne Borgo's house in Paris only to unwind. Her house (40 rue Jasmine) is a penthouse on the eighth floor of a grand 400-year-old building from where you get a 360 degree view of the whole city of Paris. I often get lost in my fantasies while watching the twinkling lights of the Eiffel Tower every hour or two while sipping evening tea or wine. Then the fun and frolic would begin on the streets of Paris starting with late night partying at Umesh Bhatt and his nephew Shyam Mishra's 'Namo Puja' restaurant in Strasbourg St Denis's Indian street. Umesh Bhatt is an encyclopedia on France. The films in the 'Un Certain Regard' section that one may have missed at the Cannes Film Festival can be watched again at the 'Medici Cinema' in Paris. From there I come to London for a couple of months to live with my elder brother, Mr. Tejendra Sharma. From London, sometimes I also travel to some of the other countries in Europe. As soon as I reached London, I called up Gopichand Hinduja's personal secretary, Sharmili, and introduced myself and told her that I wanted to meet Mr. Hinduja. Since I had not been introduced to Sharmili, she obviously wouldn't have given any special importance to my phone call. She asked me to call after a week or ten days because Gopichand Hinduja was travelling. So, I also went for a countryside tour of Ireland and Wales with my friend Nikhil Kaushik. On the morning of June 20, when I called Sharmili, she said that Gopichand Hinduja was very busy and would only be able to meet me after a week. I requested her to convey my message to Gopichand Hinduja ji. In the evening, a call came from a private number wherein the caller's phone number was not displayed. When I picked up the phone, Sharmili was on the line. She said—"Mr. Rai, can you come to our office at New Zealand House tomorrow at five o'clock?" I immediately said, "Yes," and wrote down the address. I can surmise that when Sharmili would have presented the list of those seeking an appointment with Gopichand Hinduja, he would have asked her to call me immediately. Earlier, Rakesh Mathur had intimidated me by telling me that Gopichand Hinduja wasn't very fond of journalists. Recently, he had refused to give interviews to the Sunday Times and BBC reporters. When I told Rakesh Mathur about my meeting with Gopichand Hinduja, he did not believe me. He said that the Sunday Times had slightly manipulated the assessment of his wealth in the past and placed him at number two on the list of the richest people in the UK. Later, in the next assessment, he was again placed at number one. So, in this way, the meeting which was to be held after a week happened in a day.

After returning to India, when I went to Mumbai, I met Ashish Ahuja, and Ashok Parmanand Hinduja, the youngest of the Hinduja brothers, on 12 September, 2017 at Hinduja House situated at 171, Annie Besant Marg, Worli. I was happy to know that he too, like the rest of the Hinduja brothers, was very cheerful and polite. Mangesh Bansod, director of the Academy of Theater Arts at the University of Mumbai, had invited me to teach world cinema and theatre. Ashish Ahuja wanted to know whether enough material was available on the subject that a book could be written. So far we had reached only an in-principle agreement. Ashish Ahuja suggested that I send him a detailed written proposal of the book on reaching Delhi as they would have to complete some legal formalities. As soon as I returned to Delhi, I got busy with my work. I got a call from Prakash Hinduja on Diwali. He asked me why I had not yet sent the book proposal to Ashish Ahuja. So, I mailed him a proposal right away. The date was 19 October, 2017. It was only two years later that finally with the efforts of Ashish Ahuja, on 26 September, 2019, I signed a legal contract to write the book at the Hinduja House in Mumbai. I must admit here that Ashish Ahuja helped me in every way possible. There were several sessions of 'Walk and Talk' in the mornings during November-December, 2019. On 20 March, 2020, a plane ticket to Jaipur and from there to Mumbai was also booked. One day, suddenly, I came to know that all the cultural activities across the country have been suspended. The COVID-19 crisis had started and only after a few days the whole country was put under lockdown. Then the second wave hit and the visit to Mumbai kept on getting postponed.

The 71st Cannes Film Festival (8-19 May, 2018) was historic for me. That year, I set a world record in film journalism. In twelve days, I had a total of 75 articles and reports on the Cannes Film Festival published in Indian newspapers. Perhaps, this was the first time ever that 75 articles were published in twelve days on a single event by a film journalist. My aim was to get the White press card. That year, many of my favourite filmmakers' films were in the official selection. Iranian filmmaker Asghar Farhadi's Spanish film 'Everybody Knows' had opened at the 71st Cannes Film Festival. The legendary French filmmaker who is considered the God of world cinema Jean-Luc Godard's 'Image Book,' 'Shape Lifter' by Hirokazu Kore-eda of Japan (it won the Palm d'Or Award for Best Film that year), Chinese filmmaker Jia Jhanche's 'Ash is Purest White,' 'Cold War' by Pawel Palikowski (Poland), 'BlacKkKlansman' by Spike Lee (USA) who was the Jury President at the 74th Cannes Film Festival (2021), 'Capernaum' by Nadine Labaki (Lebanon), 'The Summer' by the Russian filmmaker Kirill Serebrennikov, who was under house arrest in Russia, 'Three Faces' by Jafar Panahi, who was under house arrest in Iran. There was also a lot of buzz around Indian filmmaker Nandita Das' film 'Manto' in the 'Un Certain Regard' section starring Nawazuddin Siddiqui in the lead role. This was Nawazuddin Siddiqui's seventh year at the Cannes Film Festival.

I have been constantly discussing the films getting screened at the Cannes Film Festival with Prakash Hinduja and he has always valued my opinion. This is his nobility. We spent the evening of Saturday 12th May 2018 together at Martinez Hotel and he told me many anecdotes about his childhood and youth. An interesting thing he told me that when his father Parmanand Deepchand Hinduja used to travel abroad in those days, it was difficult to get vegetarian food. His mother Jamuna Hinduja had given him an aluminum tiffin box in which, when properly closed, the rice, pulses, and vegetables in the upper parts could be cooked on low flame by burning coal in the lowest part. His father believed that one should stay away from meat, liquor, and foreign women. His family did not go to any tourist place for vacation. They used to go to Haridwar and Rishikesh. Prakash Hinduja told me that his father would tie empty canisters of 'Dalda' (a vegetable cooking oil brand) around the necks of all the brothers in Haridwar's 'Har Ki Pauri' (the famous embankment on the river Ganges) and throw them in the Ganges so that they learnt to swim.

As per my routine, I got ready early in the morning on Sunday, May 13, 2018, and went to the Grand Théâtre Lumiere to watch the first press show. That day was the premiere of my favourite filmmaker Jean-Luc Godard's film 'Image Book' followed by his press conference. His press conference was very important for me. He addressed the press conference from his home in Switzerland via smartphone.

While writing my report in the media lounge after the press conference, I got a call from Prakash Hinduja. He told me to meet Gopi at Martinez Hotel at 7 o'clock in the evening. I asked him in a hurry—"Where will I find him in the Martinez Hotel." He replied—"Don't worry, you just come there. We will find you." By then I had studied a lot about the Hinduja brothers and the Hinduja Group. I finished my work and went to the India Pavilion.

Enjoying the seaside view, I walked towards the Martinez Hotel, which is located a kilometer away from the Palais des Festivals and reached there exactly at 7 o'clock in the evening. When no one showed up there, I went to the reception and told my name and asked if the Hinduja brothers had left any message for me. The boy at the reception politely told me, "There is a yacht of the Hinduja brothers on the beach outside. Maybe they are there." As I turned, an Indian gentleman came up to me and politely asked in Hindi—"Are you Ajit Rai ji?" When I said, 'Yes,' he told me that Gopichand Hinduja would take a while to come. He asked me to follow him. After crossing several corridors, we stopped near an elevator. I saw security personnel with weapons deployed on both sides of the elevator. When we reached the first floor, I saw armed security personnel deployed there as well. At first, I didn't understand why so much security was around. We then went to a huge hall. There, a great exhibition of diamonds was on display. Models from all over the world, almost naked, were adorned with a variety of diamonds. We came out to the terrace where there was a huge bar with a wide array of different varieties of liquor. He gestured to a beautiful model and asked me what I would like to drink. I quickly said—"Scotch with ice and water." The model looked at me in surprise and muttered—"Water? I said—"Yes, please." She went and got me a large peg of scotch. I thanked her and she walked away smiling. The gentleman started talking to me. He told me, "My name is Rashmi Mehta and I live in Brussels, the capital of Belgium, and I am into the diamond business." I also learnt that his family originally hailed from Mumbai and that he was a trustee of the Lilavati Hospital, Mumbai. Then I realized that he was a billionaire whom Gopichand ji had engaged just to look after me. He ordered another peg for me and started telling me about himself. He shared that the biggest diamond trade in the world takes place in Brussels, which involves a large number of Sindhi and Gujarati people. Suddenly, he received a call and said to me, "Let's go, Gopi has arrived."After coming down, he bought me chocolates and said that chocolates from Brussels are famous all over the world. Downstairs in the restaurant, Prakash Hinduja, Gopichand Hinduja, Sanjay Jumani, and many others were waiting for us. Gopichand Hinduja asked Rashmi Mehta what gift he had given me. When he came to know that he had gifted me chocolates, he said—"Oh man, you should have bought a diamond necklace for his wife." He then asked me—"What would you like to drink?" I had already drunk two large pegs of scotch. So, I said, "Coffee with milk." People laughed. Gopichand ji ordered a cappuccino for me and espresso without milk and sugar for himself. We started discussing cinema. He said that they started showing Hindi films in Iran for two reasons. First, it would promote Indian culture. Second, Indian people there would be entertained. He got nostalgic and started humming a song from the Manoj Kumar film 'Purab Aur Paschim'—"Koi Jab Tumhara Hriday Tod De, Tadapta Hua Jab Tumhe Chhod De, Tab Tum Mere Paas Aana Priye, Mera Dar Khula Hai Khula Hee Rahega Tumhare Liyein..."

That year there was a death in the Hinduja family or of a close relative of theirs. Therefore, the Indian vegetarian dinner, usually held during the Cannes Film Festival, did not take place that year. Gopichand Hinduja left for London. Before leaving, he told me—"If you come to London this time, then you must come to our house." Three days later, on the morning of 16 May 2018, Prakash Hinduja told me that in the evening on his yacht he would be hosting a party for me, which would also have some foreign guests. Again, the same problem presented itself—how would I reach his yacht? He understood my dilemma and said—"You please come to Martinez Hotel. From there my driver will bring you to the yacht." That's what happened. When I reached his yacht, he was waiting for me there. Filmmakers, producers, and industrialists from many countries were already present there. Prakash Hinduja, as always, introduced me as the most important film journalist from India. For about an hour, I kept answering the questions of those foreign guests. An English waitress came and asked me—"What would you like to drink?" I wanted to know about the available options. She gestured for me to come with her. We went down the stairs to the basement and she opened the bar door. I saw that there were many bottles of choicest liquor stacked one after the other. I put my finger on the Johnnie Walker Blue Label and came back upstairs. After the banquet, Prakash Hinduja dropped me in his car to my apartment. During the feast, he reiterated that India could very easily become a world power in the field of cinema. He also said that when S. M. Khan was the Director-General of the Directorate of Film Festivals, he had made him meet the people of UniFrance, the famous institution of cinema in France, in Cannes. Malti Sahay was also there in that meeting. UniFrance is a government trust that finances young French filmmakers to make good films. A part (perhaps ten or twenty percent) of the income that the government gets from cinema in the form of tax from all over the country is given by UniFrance the form of grant. Prakash Hinduja said that the Indian government should also do the same. He had a suggestion and he has told me many times that Jill Jacob, who has established the Cannes Film Festival, must be invited by the Government of India to the Goa Film Festival, and the Indian people should learn from him. Jill Jacob has written a book in French on the history of the Cannes Film Festival. Marianne Borgo showed me that book. I could not tell Prakash Hinduja that the present Government in India and its officials are not interested in all these meaningful works. They merely follow a ritualistic approach without any concrete plans in place. However, I noticed that Prakash Hinduja had an abundance of ideas and information about cinema. Like every year, after the Cannes Film Festival ended, I came to Paris with Marianne Borgo.

While walking down the Champs-Élysées, the most beautiful street in Paris, my friend Anju Bala Probst suggested—"This time, you should travel to London by bus." I too liked the idea as I would be able to see the countryside of France and England. I often travel from Paris to London by train or plane. Anju herself booked the ticket and she also brought potato stuffed parathas (a filling Indian snack) to be eaten on the way. I take great thrill in crossing the border of two countries via land. I wanted to see how the bus from under the sea would cross the English Channel to reach London. It was the same border that innumerable people have been killed trying to cross. There has been enmity between England and France for the last four hundred years. Many films have been shot on this border. Thinking of all this, I fell asleep.

When I opened my eyes, I found my bus had stopped at a red light and a tape was playing at a general store outside and it was in Mehdi Hassan Sahab's voice—"Duniya Kisi Ke Pyar Mein Jannat Se Nahi Kam Hai."(The world is no less than heaven when one is in love with someone). My heart became romantic and countless memories of my love affairs came back to me at that moment. I thought I had reached London. This shop must be of some Lahori (Pakistani) from where the sound of Mehdi Hassan's song was coming. I did the right thing by following the advice of Anju Bala Probst. The bus was destined for the Victoria Bus Station in London. I had two heavy suitcases, two bags, and a handbag. It would have been very difficult to walk to the Victoria Underground Metro Station with so much luggage. I had taken a taxi from Marianne Borgo's house in Paris to catch the bus to London. From Victoria, I had to take the train to Harrow and Wealdstone. With so much luggage, the train had to be changed at one point in the middle. Tejendra, my brother, had explained everything clearly in writing. When I arrived at Harrow and Wealdstone, I saw that he had hired a taxi for me which drove me to his home, 33A Spencer Road, for just 5 pounds. It was eleven o'clock in the night. The arrival of Tejendra Sharma and Zakia Zubairy in my life is nothing short of a miracle. I will write a separate book on it some other time. Today, the whole world is under my feet, and all this has been made possible only because of an elder brother like Tejendra Sharma. First of all, in 2007, he opened the world's first window for me. My first meeting with him and Counselor Zakia Zubairy was on January 17, 2007, at the Indian High School at the Second World Hindi Conference of the Gulf Countries. The night was passing by and the pages of the glorious history of Hindi cinema were shining in front of me from which Bollywood was established. It was the dreamy night of Monday, 28 May. Recalling the famous Hindi writer Kamleshwar's book 'Mumbai Raat Ki Baahon Mein (Mumbai, In the Arms of Night),' I thought that one day I would also write a book 'London Raat Bhar (London, All Night Long).'

The next week in London was spent with Rakesh Mathur in the world of art, culture, and literature. Jaipur Literature Festival and Arundhati Roy at the British Library, Shashi Tharoor's lectures at the London School of Economics, Reception at Asia House, meeting with the High Commissioner of the Indian High Commission, conversations on Indian politics and cinema with several MPs at the House of Lords, the Upper House of the British Parliament, spending time in Abid Gulzar's company in Eastbourne along with Nikhil Kaushik and

Dev Anand with Srichand Hinduja

waiting for a call from Prakash Hinduja. On the 8th of June, Prakash Hinduja called, and asked me to come to St James's Park near Buckingham Palace the next morning at exactly eight o'clock. He said that he, Gopichand Hinduja, and many other friends take a walk there for an hour. He asked me to wait near the canteen. The next morning, I hurriedly got ready to reach the canteen at St. James's Park, but I was an hour late. So, I called Prakash Hinduja back. He asked me to come home. I was wandering around near his house but could not find it. That's when I saw Prakash Hinduja himself come out looking for me. He took me to 13—16 Carlton House Terrace, where the Hinduja brothers live. This house previously belonged to Britain's Queen Victoria. A life-size marble statue of Queen Victoria stands outside the building. As soon as you enter the building, the idols of Lakshmi, Ganesha, and Saraswati greet you in the front where a lamp is kept lit. They took me to an inner room, a sort of golden room, where sixteen people can have breakfast together at a huge table placed there. The room was decorated in gold design in every way. The walls, photo frames, chairs, tables, and everything seem to be studded with gold. He lovingly served me an Indian vegetarian breakfast and tea. Soon, Gopichand Hinduja also joined us. I still remember what Gopichand Hinduja said to me that day, "Son, today I can buy everything, but I cannot buy time."

We decided that while I was in London, I would be walking for an hour every morning, from 8 to 9, in St. James' Park with Gopichand Hinduja while talking about the global cultural journey of Hindi cinema. This routine continued till 27 June 2018.

It has always been my dream to wake up at 4 in the morning which is seldom possible. In London, this became possible every day, together with my elder brother, Tejendra Sharma's tea and biscuits. He would wake up at 3.30 am to go for his morning duty. He would wake me up at 4 o'clock after readying tea for me. His taxi would arrive at 4:40 am and he would leave. For the morning walk with Gopichand Hinduja, I had to leave home at 6.30 am to take the 6.56 Bakerloo line train from Harrow and Wildstone railway station to reach Piccadilly Circus at 7.35 am. From there, I used to walk to St. James Park Cafe where we would meet outside at 7.50 am. Gopichand Hinduja would always have a bag in his hand, filled with pieces of bread, peanuts, gram, etc., which we would feed to ducks, crows, pigeons, and squirrels. An hour would fly by during which we would cover four to five kilometers walking. Often, he would narrate anecdotes making me laugh endlessly. At 8.50 am, we used to have coffee at a café there. He preferred black espresso coffee without milk and sugar whereas I would have cappuccino with milk and croissant. Exactly at 9.05 am, we would get up. I could have never imagined that the richest man in Britain would be so humble and sweet. Even at the age of eighty, he is fitter and healthier than me. Every day while walking he would narrate to me fascinating anecdotes of the last sixty years, from Raj Kapoor's 'Sangam' to Amitabh Bachchan's 'Coolie.' While talking, he would often get lost in old memories and start singing songs. His favourite song is "Ae Malik Tere Bande Hum" (O Lord, We Are Your Servants) from V. Shantaram's film 'Do Aankhen Barah Haath'. During the walk, we used to be accompanied by businessmen from many countries as well as many capitalists from India and Britain. I learned a lot while walking with him. Some of the things, I cannot even write here. He used to tell me time and again—"You are comfortable eating egg and omelet and so please don't hesitate to eat it on my account." Many times, he would bring an Indian vegetarian breakfast for me from his home. Once he told me to take it home and also share it with my elder brother Tejendra Sharma. One day we met a young astrologer named Sandeep Kochhar. On that day also he had got packed potato stuffed parathas vegetable curry, and semolina pudding for me. We all went to his house. There he wanted to know something about Indian astrology from Sandeep Kochhar. When we started walking, he gave me my food packet and said—"It slipped my mind, I should have got food packed for Sandeep too. But it doesn't matter. My mother used to say—'Son, whatever food you have, share it and eat it.' So, you both please share the meal." I ate that meal sharing it with Sandeep Kochhar while sitting on a bench at the Trafalgar Square. Pigeons were flying all around us. Once Gopichand Hinduja had to leave a little early and so he asked a gentleman to take me along with him, instructing him to take proper care of me. When I started walking with that gentleman, he narrated to me many tales. His name was Prakash Lohia. He was the Chairman of the multinational company, Indorama. I discovered that he was the fifth richest citizen of Britain. During our meetings, Gopichand Hinduja narrated the entire story of Hindi cinema in Iran which has been covered in detail in the coming chapters. He would ask me again and again—"Son, what can I do for you?" I would answer every time—"I don't want anything. Your blessings are my wealth." One day he told me—"I have seen many types of journalists and it is also true that I do not like journalists, but, son, I have fallen in love with you. If there's anything that I can do for you, please don't ever hesitate to say it."

This routine of meeting Gopichand and Prakash Hinduja continued. There was only one hesitation in their minds about the book. That it should not be misunderstood that they are getting me to write something in their praise or are spreading their propaganda. I cleared their doubts by assuring them that the book would not be about just one person or family. It would be a collective history of many different anecdotes and perspectives. That's how a whole year passed.

We met again at the 72nd Cannes Film Festival (14-25 May 2019). This time on the morning of May 20, 2019, Gopichand Hinduja and I met once again for breakfast at 72 Crochet Cafe. We talked about a whole lot of things and promised to meet up in London again. Then on the evening of 22 May, Prakash Hinduja organized a dinner for me on his yacht 'Param Jamuna'. The yacht is named 'Param Jamuna' by the Hinduja brothers after their father Parmanand

and mother Jamuna. I would never be ableto forget that incredible evening. This time he himself dropped me in his car at my apartment. Earlier on 13 May 2019, the London newspaper Sunday Times, correcting its previous assessment, declared the Hinduja brothers as the richest citizens of Britain. Newspapers all around the world published—Indian-born Gopichand Hinduja becomes Britain's richest for the third time—Hinduja brothers (Srichand—Gopichand) are at number one in the list of richest British people released by Sunday Times (London). In 2014 and 2017 also, he was number one. His net worth was estimated at 22 billion pounds (over two lakh crore rupees). This time when I met him in London, he was in a great mood. He made me listen to many songs of his choice and phoned Ashish Ahuja to give him the green signal for the book. One day at my behest, he called up Boris Johnson. Till then Johnson had not become the Prime Minister of Britain but was about to be. Gopichand Hinduja told him—"When you become the Prime Minister, then please treat my boys at 10 Downing Street (Prime Minister's residence) to tea." Boris Johnson happily agreed. Similarly, he told me many political stories associated with Sh. Morarji Desai, Smt. Indira Gandhi, Sh. Rajiv Gandhi, Sh. Giani Zail Singh, Sh. Sharad Pawar, etc. Gopichand ji and Prakash ji stayed in Mumbai for several weeks in December. During that time, I used to meet them every day. They used to be accompanied by Ashok Hinduja. For the first time in the company of the Hinduja brothers, I was falling in love with Mumbai.

I went to Mumbai (then Bombay) for the first time on 12 October 1993. At the Indian Express office at Nariman Point,I had met Dhirendra Asthana, the editor of the Sunday supplement 'Sabrang' of Jansatta and my favourite storyteller. I still remember meeting Dharamveer Bharti ji, former editor of Dharmayug, at Sehwas Apartment. After that, I kept coming to Mumbai regularly. My friend Nilay Upadhyay had also left Bihar and settled in Mumbai. When Vaman Kendra became the director of the Academy of Theater Arts, Mumbai University, he started inviting me to teach Hindi theater and cinema there. I missed many opportunities to work and live in Mumbai because first, I don't know why, I don't like the crowds and fast-paced life of Mumbai, and, second, I was scared of Mumbai. Whenever I would go to Mumbai, I would always try to escape to Delhi soon.

I wrote in my diary on 10th December 2019 that for the first time I was falling in love with Mumbai. This was the first time I was in Mumbai for such a long time. There were so many stories getting scattered around me. Stories of Gopichand, Prakash, and Ashok Hinduja, wherein there were many untold episodes of Hindi cinema. While working with the Hinduja family, I started looking at this city with love. After the morning walk at Juhu beach and a visit to the Hare Krishna ISKCON Temple, a new world would open up before me during the discussions at the Hinduja Bungalow. The company of Prakash Hinduja is pleasantly wonderful. The opportunity to write a book on the global cultural journey of twelve hundred Hindi films was no less than a boon. I was falling in love with Mumbai. I was staying at my old friend Mukul Anand's Oshiwara apartment under the care of theater artist Ajay Kumar. Interestingly, at the same time, the routine of London had started again. Waking up at 4 AM, getting ready to leave for Hinduja Bungalow, then Param Plaza, at 6.30 AM, and 'walk and talk' at the Juhu Beach from 7 to 8 AM, and back at nine o'clock after breakfast. One day something amazing happened. I was recording the memoirs of those days while walking as usual on the Juhu beach with Gopichand, Prakash, and Ashok Hinduja. Soon, ten to twelve people joined us. Gopichand asked Ashok Hinduja in front of everyone—"Ashok if you allow me, and if you can make the necessary arrangements, then I would like all of them to come home and have breakfast with us." Ashok shrugged and said—"Why do you need permission? Just bring all of them home." We had reached the place where our cars would usually be parked. Gopichand Hinduja took us all and came to the main road. He noticed that there were just two cars and twelve people in total. He suggested I hire three or four auto rickshaws as it would take a lot of time to get more vehicles from home. He sent some people to the house in the two available cars and sat with me in an auto rickshaw. Sitting in the auto rickshaw, I was looking at another Gopichand Hinduja. Britain's richest man, who has no shortage of private jets, was traveling with me in a simple auto rickshaw on the streets of Mumbai.

3

When Raj Kapoor was Pulled Out of Tehran's Theatre in a Prison Car

The story begins at the start of World War I, when a 13-year-old boy traveled from Shikarpur city in Sindh (now in Pakistan) to Bombay (now Mumbai). He carried with him the legacy of the five thousand years old great Indus Valley Civilization, when the first lessons of organized trade and banking were learnt by humans on this earth. The boy's name was Parmanand Deepchand Hinduja (1901–71). He along with his wife Jamuna Parmanand Hinduja laid the foundation of the great Hinduja Group which today is one of the largest role models of value-based business in the whole world. He formulated and adopted five important principles of business and stuck to those principles throughout his life. Today, even after a hundred years, the Hinduja Group is running on the same principles—

1. He believed that "my Dharma (duty) is to work and so that I can give something back to the society." The first principle revolves around the idea of "work to give," which emphasizes the importance to work so that we can give something back to others and society.
2. The second principle was—"Work is a bond," i.e. the world trusts our work. People's trust should be our capital.
3. The third principle, "Act Local, Think Global," means that no matter how international we become, we must always take care of the local people.
4. The fourth principle, "Partnership for Growth," means that we have to make internal and external partnerships for development so that we can work and grow together.
5. The fifth principle, "Advance fearlessly," emphasizes moving forward without fear. Parmanand Deepchand Hinduja and Jamuna Parmanand Hinduja had five children—Girdhar Parmanand Hinduja (1932–1962), Srichand Parmanand Hinduja (1935), Gopichand Parmanand Hinduja (1940), Prakash Parmanand Hinduja (1945), and Ashok Parmanand Hinduja (1950).

After the end of World War I, in the year 1919, Parmanand Deepchand Hinduja opened his business office in Tehran, the capital of Iran. It was the first foreign trading office of an Indian industrialist at that time. It is also surprising that an 18-year-old Indian went out of India at that time and laid the foundation of the Hinduja Group in an Islamic country like Iran. He sent one of his brothers to Afghanistan to do business and sent another brother to Karachi. With his hard work and dedication, he earned one crore rupees in 1921. Adjusting for inflation, it can be easily guessed what would be the actual worth of one crore rupees at that time. The year 2021 marked its centenary.

Prakash, Srichand, Gopichand, and Ashok Hinduja

Later, when his business picked up, Parmanand Hinduja called his eldest son Girdhar Hinduja (1932–1962) from Mumbai to Tehran. At that time a large number of Indians worked in Iran. It was a foreign country with a different culture and so Girdhar Hinduja thought of bringing Hindi films there so that Indians would be entertained and the Indian culture would also get promoted. Girdhar Hinduja engaged his other brother Srichand Hinduja in this work in Mumbai. Karan Johar's company Dharma Productions is named after Srichand's son Dharam Hinduja. Karan Johar's father Yash Johar had already worked with the Hinduja brothers. Subsequently, hewas working for Vijay Anand's Navketan Films and used to help in the production. When he wanted to leave Navketan in order to start his own film production business, he requested Srichand Hinduja for some financial help and Srichand Hinduja immediately gave him the money. For this reason, he named his film production company Dharma Productions after Dharam Hinduja, son of Srichand Hinduja. The first film he made under the banner of Dharma Productions was 'Dostana' with Amitabh Bachchan. It was a super hit at that time, and it made tremendous profits. That's how Yash Johar's film business was established.

Ashok Hinduja, the youngest of the Hinduja brothers, used to assist in the Hinduja film business from Mumbai. Later, Gopichand Hinduja and Prakash Hinduja, took over the Iranian operations. Srichand was a friend of Raj Kapoor.It is also interesting that Parmanand Hinduja was against the business of cinema. Like Mahatma Gandhi, he also believed that cinema spoils people, makes them corrupt, and adulterous, apart from taking to drinking. He made his sons take an oath that they would never do anything wrong while engaging in the business of cinema and would always stay away from alcohol, meat, and adultery. And, the Hinduja brothers never broke their father's trust.

Girdhar Parmanand Hinduja, the eldest son of Parmanand Deepchand Hinduja, wanted to promote the Indian culture in Iran. He felt that Hindi films could become the medium as they would serve the purpose of entertainment as well as the propagation of Indian culture. At that time Raj Kapoor's film 'Shree 420' (1955) was creating a lot of buzz. The Hinduja brothers bought its rights for five thousand rupees with a minimum guarantee and released it in Iran with Persian subtitles.

Parmanand Hinduja with Raj Kapoor and others

What we call the Golden Age of Hindi cinema was also the golden age of the global cultural journey of Hindi films across the globe. Today, Hindi films are doing good business all over the world, but its foundation was laid in 1955 by the Hinduja brothers in Iran. Starting with Iran, Hindi cinema became popular all over the world. Today, hardly anyone would believe that about fifty years ago, when Raj Kapoor's film 'Sangam' was released in Iran, dubbed in Persian, it ran in the theatres for three years. It ran successfully in Cairo, the capital of Egypt, for one whole year. Indian industrialists Hinduja brothers did not just screen 'Sangam' but they screened around 1200 Hindi films worldwide and that's how 'Bollywood' came to be.

Owner of Tehran's Studio Iran being welcomed during his first visit to India. He is accompanied by Gopichand and his father Parmanand Deepchand Hinduja. The editing of Hindi films used to take place at Studio Iran

There is a very strange anecdote associated with the premiere of Raj Kapoor's film 'Shree 420' in Tehran. With great difficulty, Srichand Parmanand Hinduja had persuaded Raj Kapoor to travel to Iran (Tehran). He picked him up in his car from his office at R. K. Studio in Chembur and left for airport. En route, Raj Kapoor stated that owing to some problem in his house, he wouldn't be able to go to Iran. Actually, there were tensions in his family over his relationship with the then famous actress Nargis. Particularly, it had taken its toll on the relationship between Raj Kapoor and his wife Krishna Kapoor. By then he already had two children and he was not ready to leave his wife Krishna Kapoor and the two children—Randhir Kapoor and Rishi Kapoor—and marry Nargis. Madhu Jain, who wrote the famous book 'The Kapoors—The First Family of Indian Cinema' on the Kapoor family, told BBC's Rehan Fazal, "Nargis had given her heart, her soul to Raj Kapoor; she had also started investing her money in Raj Kapoor's films. When R. K. Studios was short of money, Nargis even sold her gold bangles. She even did films for other producers such as 'Adalat,' 'Ghar,' 'Sansar,' and 'Lajwanti' in order to financially support R. K. Films.Raj Kapoor later made a famous but insensitive remark about her, "My wife is the mother of my children, but Nargis is the mother of my films."

Raj Kapoor's wife Krishna Kapoor had told Bunny Reuben that after separating with Nargis, Raj Kapoor used to return home very late and this continued for many nights. He had started drinking heavily. He used to lie down in his bathtub and cry endlessly. I knew that he was crying for Nargis.

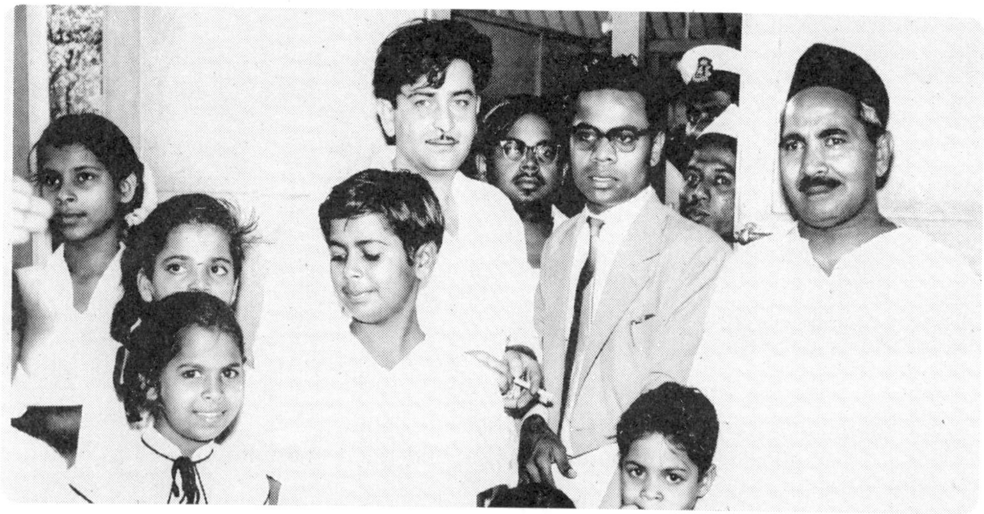

Raj Kapoor, Parmanand Hinduja, and other Members of the Family

Senior BBC journalist Rehan Fazal writes that Raj Kapoor had a very special relationship with alcohol. Once Raj Kapoor's elder son, Randhir Kapoor, told Rehan Fazal that Raj Kapoor would always drink Johnnie Walker Black Label whiskey bought from London. Madhu Jain, in her book 'The Kapoors - The First Family of Indian Cinema,' quotes his younger son Rishi Kapoor saying, "Raj

Kapoor used to be very possessive about his Black Label whiskey. Even when he used to go to parties he used to take his favourite liquor along with him. Even in sharing liquor, he followed a certain kind of caste system. He himself used to drink Black Label bought from London and would share it only with a very few special friends.''

Madhu Jain further writes, "Tanuja was amongst those few very special friends. Black Label whisky purchased from Dubai was meant for his other friends and finally, Black Label whisky purchased from Delhi and Mumbai was meant for his sons. Randhir Kapoor used to feel very bad that Tanuja would get to drink the whiskey from London while he would get to drink the locally purchased whisky."

Rehan Fazal writes that Raj Kapoor was a great host. When he used to host parties, he would ensure that the menu offered a wide variety of cuisines for his guests to choose from. But he himself used to eat very less. His favourite meal used to be pav, egg with some pulses. For years after separating from Nargis, he did not eat food during the day, and even at night when he used to return very late, he would only eat fried eggs before going to bed. He always used to travel by his Ambassador car even though he had a Mercedes, which was only used by his wife Krishna Kapoor.

It created a very difficult situation for everyone when Raj Kapoor said that he would not be able to go to Tehran. All the preparations for the premiere of the film had been done in Iran. Somehow Srichand ji persuaded Raj Kapoor to go to Tehran. Raj Kapoor insisted that Srichand would have to drink alcohol with him on the plane. Raj Kapoor knew that Srichand Hinduja did not drink alcohol. In those days there was no direct flight to Iran and so they had to go via Karachi (Pakistan). By the time the plane reached Karachi, Raj Kapoor had drunk so much that he needed support to get off the plane. Srichand was very concerned because a huge crowd of Pakistanis had gathered at the Karachi Airport to see Raj Kapoor. However, the next morning Raj Kapoor apologized to Srichand for his behaviour.

Raj Kapoor at the marriage ceremony of Srichand and Gopichand Hinduja

'Shree 420' was released for the first time in Tehran's 'Cinema Iran'. Later, a huge crowd gathered at the film's premiere at the 'Kucha-e-Lalzar' cinema. When Raj Kapoor came on stage in a blue suit and red tie, the Iranians thought a Russian had arrived. Raj Kapoor had become a superstar in Iran after the film's show. He was surrounded by a crowd of fans. The crowd started getting uncontrollable. Finally, the police had to be called. With great difficulty, he was taken out from the back door in an armored vehicle used for carrying the prisoners to the jail. 'Shree 420' ran very well in Iran. Today, it is hard to believe that the film 'Shri 420' successfully ran for a year and a half in 'Hafiz' cinema in Tehran. The company made a lot of profit. Then Raj Kapoor's first film 'Aag' (1948) was released, but it was less successful. Dev Anand and Geeta Bali's 'Baazi' was also very successful. This trend went on successfully as the Hinduja group screened about twelve hundred Hindi films in different countries outside India and not even a single film suffered any loss.

At that time the upper class in Tehran only went to watch Hollywood movies. Hollywood movies used to run only for four-five or six days at best. The reason being, the number of upper-class patrons was very less. Hindi cinema connected with the general Iranian audiences. Habib Malik, the owner of 'Shahbaz' cinema, had become crazy about Hindi cinema. With great difficulty, he would agree to take down the film whose run had completed.

Srichand Hinduja, Sunil Dutt with his wife Nargis Dutt and son Sanjay Dutt (in his arms)

Encouraged by the phenomenal success of Hindi films in Iran, Girdhar Parmanand Hinduja decided to dub them into Persian and release them. He tied up with Filmistan Studio in Bombay. It was the beginning of a new era. In a way, the post-mortem or dissection of the entire Hindi film would result in a completely new version for the Iranian audience. Sometimes even the titles and dialogues of films were changed. For example, the film 'Durgesh Nandini' was released in Iran under the title 'Akbar-e-Huqam'. Almost all the big Hindi films of that time were released in Iran. Inspired by the success in Iran, Girdhar Parmanand Hinduja released Hindi films in other countries like Jordan, Egypt, Lebanon, Greece, etc.

Sunil Dutt and Nargis came to Tehran for the premiere of 'Mother India'. At that time Nargis had become a superstar in Iran. The Iranian people were desperate to get a glimpse of her but no one knew Sunil Dutt. When they came to the cinema hall for the premiere, Nargis was surrounded by the Iranians but no one paid any importance to Sunil Dutt. This made him very upset. Girdhar Hinduja then sat down with him, giving him company, and kept him engaged in conversation.

It is said that the worldwide popularity of Raj Kapoor started in Iran. The credit for this goes to the Hinduja brothers. This is a history that has not been written anywhere till date. The second part of this story began when, exactly ten years after the film 'Shree 420', in the presence of Raj Kapoor, his next film 'Sangam', dubbed in Persian, got released in Iran in October 1964.

RAM
SHYAM

4

Raj Kapoor's film 'Sangam' ran for Three Years at Tehran's Hafiz Cinema

Seeing the photographs of Raj Kapoor, Nargis, and Vyjayanthimala next to the photographs of the Hollywood stalwarts—Elizabeth Taylor and Ingrid Bergman—in the world famous Cinema Museum of Tehran, it can be easily guessed how influential Hindi cinema would have been in the country atone point in time.The photos displayed in the 'Museum of Memories' section are from the time when Raj Kapoor and Nargis visited Iran at the invitation of the Hinduja brothers and went to Tehran's Central Studio with Iranian superstars Gogoosh and Mahvash. London-based Iranian writer and filmmaker Ehsan Khoshbakht has written in the famous cinema magazine 'Sight and Sound' that in the fifties Raj Kapoor was a household name in Iran and during that period about 49 Hindi films had got released in the cinema halls across the countrywhich had dented the market of Hollywood films, drastically. Famous Iranian film expert Hameed Raza Sadr had written that Raj Kapoor, Nargis, Vyjayanthimala, and other film actors often visited Iran for the premiere of their films. But they do not explain how this magic happened. Not only in Iran but all over the world in the fifties-sixties, this magic was created by the Hinduja brothers.

The Hinduja brothers took Raj Kapoor to Tehran's most elite cinema hall 'Saadi' and screened 'Sangam' in October 1964. 'Sangam' went housefull for three weeks. But its owner was not very happy. He came to Gopichand Hinduja and told him that he was discontinuing the screening as it was not going well with his Hollywood film viewing patrons,which, in turn, could badly affect his business. Gopichand Hinduja spent a sleepless night because of it. The next morning, he went to meet the owner of 'Hafiz,' the cinema hall right across 'Saadi'. A Hollywood film, 'Four Horses,' was being screened there. The owner said that the business was not doing well and the money position was tight. Gopichand Hinduja gave him a loan of ten lakh rupees on the condition that he would screen their Hindi films in 'Hafiz'. He was overjoyed. That very day, he dropped the Hollywood film 'Four Horses' and started screening 'Sangam' from the 3 o'clock show onwards. This event was seen by Indians as the victory of Hindi cinema over Hollywood.'Sangam' went on to create a record there by running continuously for three years. The film also did well in Beirut's 'Rivoli' cinema and Israel's 'Eden' cinema. 'Sangam' was also screened at the Cannes Film Festival that year. At that time the Hinduja brothers had bought the international rights of 'Sangam' from Raj Kapoor for one lakh British pounds. Back then one British pound was equivalent to thirteen rupees. This amount was more than four times the amount for which the international rights of Mehboob Khan's film 'Mother India' were bought.

The reason was that the promotion of Indian culture through these films was more important for the Hinduja brothers than earning money. G. P. Sippy and Ramesh Sippy's 'Sholay' and Mehboob Khan's 'Mother India' also ran successfully in Iran for a whole year. 'Sholay' remains the favourite film of Iranians even today.

The first poster of Sangam when the Hinduja Brothers had bought the international rights of the film

At that time the upper class in Tehran only used to watch Hollywood movies. Hollywood movies used to run only four-five or six days. The reason was that the number of upper-class patronswas very small. Hindi cinema, on the other hand, connected with the common Iranian audience. It is evident from the fact that cinema owners such as Habib Malik, who used to run 'Shahbaz' cinema, had become so fascinated with Hindi cinema that they had to be convinced with great difficulty to take down a Hindi film even after it had completed a very successful run.

Prakash Hinduja, Chairman (Europe), Hinduja Udyog Group, says, "We opened a dubbing office at Filmistan Studio in Mumbai where we used to dub all Hindi films in Persian. Filmistan Studio was owned by Tolaram Jalan. We talked to him. Several times we used to even change the name of the film. We also used to change the dialogues of the film. We used to call artists from Iran whose voices were similar to Indian artists. Today, if you watch those dubbed prints then you might be surprised to see Raj Kapoor, Dev Anand, Dilip Kumar, etc. delivering dialogues in Persian. Not only this, we typically used to edit an 18-20 reels long film to about 10-12 reels long film. Gopichand Hinduja had become an expert in editing the films."

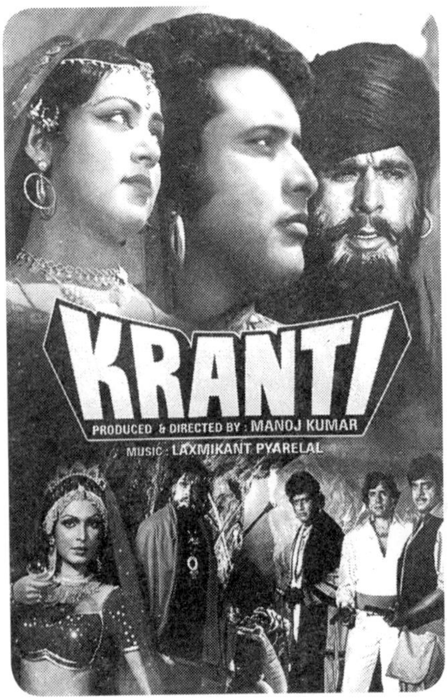

"Gopichand Hinduja cut down 'Sangam' from four hours to two hours in the Persian version without telling Raj Kapoor. At its premiere in Tehran, Srichand Hinduja had managed to bring Raj Kapoor. We were all scared that he might get angry to see the edited version. The film premiered in the evening. In the balcony of the theater, Srichand sat on one side of Raj Kapoor and Gopi on the other side. Raj Kapoor kept watching the film silently while drinking his Scotch which we had got for him especially from London. As soon as the film was over, he got up and hugged Gopi and said that he couldn't have done such a good job of editing himself."

When I came to London on my way back from the 71st Cannes Film Festival (2018), I followed a daily 'walk and talk' routine with the Hinduja Group Co-Chairman Gopichand Hinduja in the month of June at St. James's Park. During this, he disclosed many things which have not come to the fore to date. He said, "We used to prepare a whole new version for the Iranian audience by doing a post-mortem of the entire Hindi film. Sometimes even the names of the films and the dialogues were changed. For example, the 1956 film 'Durgesh Nandini'was released in Iran under the name 'Farman-e-Akbar'. Similarly, Dev Anand's 'Guide' was titled 'Rahnuma'. We released almost all the big films of that time in Iran. Inspired by the success of Iran, we released Hindi films in other countries like Jordan, Egypt, Lebanon, Syria, Greece, Thailand, Israel, Turkey etc."

Gopichand Hinduja shared that Yash Chopra's film 'Dhool Ka Phool' (1959) had a great run in India. It starred Rajendra Kumar, Mala Sinha, and Nanda in the lead roles. But the film did not play even for a day in Iran. After three years they changed some parts of the film and released it. In countries where they had good partners, their business did really well. For example, they were very successful in Jordan, Egypt, Beirut, Iraq, etc. But their partner in Turkey turned out to be wrong and hence they had to replace him.

Gopichand Hinduja continued, "People repeatedly ask us why we closed down the cinema business. I just tell them that the times had changed. There were two reasons for closing the business of cinema. First,our business had grown so much that we did not have the time we had earlier. Second, gradually some very different types of people started entering the business of cinema.For them earning money somehow became the main aim. People like Raj Kapoor, Dev Anand, Dilip Kumar, and Manoj Kumar are rare. For these people, country and society were more important than money. The general public used to take pride in them. Today the new breed of actors is a little different. So, we sold all our business related to cinema in 1978. However, even later on we continued to help many filmmakers."

Raj Kapoor with Parmanand Hinduja and others in Iran on the occasion of the film premiere of 'Shree 420'

"I remember when the owner dropped Raj Kapoor's film 'Sangam' at 'Saadi' cinema in Tehran (Iran) after three weeks of running housefull, I couldn't sleep that night. The next morning, I went to meet the owner of 'Hafiz,' the cinema hall right across from 'Saadi'. A Hollywood film, 'Four Horses,' was being screened there. He told me that business was not going well and money was tight.I gave him a loan of ten lakh rupees on the condition that he would screen our Hindi films in his cinema hall 'Hafiz'. The family said that I had gone mad. What would happen if the money wasn't returned? There was 'Four Horses' during the 12 o'clock show and 'Sangam' at 3 o'clock. 'Sangam' went on to create a record there by running continuously for three years. In the adjacent cinema hall, K. Asif's film 'Mughal-e-Azam' was running."

The Hinduja brothers had become close friends with Raj Kapoor. He used to come frequently to London to meet them and do other work. He used to sit with Gopichand ji on the ground and they would talk for hours. Another famous story about Raj Kapoor is that he never slept on the bed. He always slept on the ground. He got this habit from the former President of India, Giani Zail Singh. His daughter Ritu Nanda once told BBC's Rehan Fazal—

"Raj Kapoor had the habit of sleeping on the floor.He used to drag the mattress from the bed of the hotel where he stayed and put it on the ground. Because of this, he got into trouble many times. When he did this in London's famous Hilton Hotel he was given a warning at first but when he did the same thing again, the hoteliers fined him. On that occasion, he stayed in that hotel for five days and he happily paid a daily fine for dragging the mattress on the ground."

Once, someone tried to turn Raj Kapoor against the Hinduja brothers by telling him that he wasn't given his due by the Hindujas who were taking away the lion's share of the profits. Gopichand ji says, "When I came to know about this, I was very sad and angry too. I asked Raj Kapoor to send his chartered accountant and get all the accounts checked." After a few years, Raj Kapoor realized his mistake and his relationship with the Hinduja brothers went back to normal. Now, he started taking the advice of Gopichand ji for each of his films. He made another long film in 1970 titled 'Mera Naam Joker' which had two intervals. He showed this film to Gopichand Hinduja. Immediately after watching the film, Gopichand Hinduja told him that it would not work. He told him thatit was very long and felt like a documentary. And just as Gopichand Hinduja had predicted, the film failed to create the magic of Raj Kapoor's earlier films and he suffered a huge loss because ofit. He almost went bankrupt. At that time, the Hinduja brothers not only encouraged him, but also helped him financially to make his next film 'Bobby' (1973). At that time, the Hinduja brothers gave him ten lakh rupees. Raj Kapoor's luck turned and 'Bobby' became a super-duper hit. With the profits made from the film, Raj Kapoor bought a bungalow for his wife Krishna Kapoor.

There is no denying that Raj Kapoor was known all over the world in the sixties and seventies. His popularity in Iran and Russia (Soviet Union) was as high as that of the presidents there. The songs of his films 'Shree 420,' 'Awara,' 'Mera Naam Joker,' etc. resonated all over the world. At the same time, it is also true that the Hinduja brothers played an important role in the global popularity of Raj Kapoor.

So, what was the secret behind Raj Kapoor's popularity not only in Iran and Russia but all over the world? Rehan Fazal writes that once when Raj Kapoor came to the BBC's Bush House office in London, he responded to this question by saying, "This is an anecdote from 1954 when I went to Russia with two of my photographs. One of them was from 'Awara.' This picture was my first introductionto the people of Russia. The Russians knew a little bit of India, but through these two photographs they came closer to India."

The character from 'Awara' had some similarities to Raj Kapoor's appearance, but his heart belonged to the people of India. Actually, the audiences did not adopt Raj Kapoor, they adopted the young man of India whose heart used to say this again and again—

"Aabaad Nahi, Barbaad Sahi, Gaata Hoon Khushi Ke Geet Magar

Anjaan Magar Sunsaan Dagar Ka Pyaara Hoon, Awaara Hoon!"

Or

"Mera Joota Hai Japani, Yeh Patloon Englishtani

Sar Pe Laal Topi Rusi, Phir Bhi Dil Hai Hindustani!"

Mohamed El Basosi, the head of the Egyptian government organization

Egyptian Film Center, told me last year at the 42nd Cairo International Film Festival (2-10 December 2020) that when the Hinduja brothers, in collaboration with the Egyptian government, released Raj Kapoor's film 'Sangam' in a theatre in Cairo, there was panic and craze all around. The film ran for about a year and it broke all box-office records. At that time several dozen Hindi films were screened in Egyptian cinema halls in collaboration with the Hinduja brothers' company and all made good money. After that Amitabh Bachchan emerged as a superstar here in the eighties. Later, due to various reasons, the relationship between Egyptian and Indian cinema suffered a breakdown. It is said that the biggest reason for this was that Hindi films had started destroying the local business revolving around the Arab cinema.

The scene is still fresh in the mind of Intishal Al Timimi, director of the El Guna Film Festival (Egypt) when the Russians had started dancing merrily, holding the car driving Shashi Kapoor and Shammi Kapoor in their hands at the Tashkent Film Festival (1983). It was no less than a dream for Timimi to meet these two great actors from India. It was enough for the Russians to know that the Kapoor brothers were actually the younger brothers of Raj Kapoor, whom the Russians consider to be the God of cinema.

Senior BBC journalist Rehan Fazal writes a story which is repeatedly told about Raj Kapoor that when India's first Prime Minister Pandit Jawaharlal Nehru went to Russia in the fifties, the Russian Prime Minister Nikolai Bulganin, during a government banquet, surprised his ministers by singing "Awaara Hoon". In 1996, when Raj Kapoor's son Randhir Kapoor and daughter Ritu Nanda went to China, their eyes filled with tears when theChinese people started singing "Awaara Hoon" on seeing them. They did not know that they were thechildren of Raj Kapoor, but they were honoring Raj Kapoor and India by singing this song. It is also said that 'Awaara' was Mao Zedong's favourite film.

Raj Kapoor's daughter Ritu Nanda told Rehan Fazal, "When Russian President Boris Yeltsin came to India in 1993 and he was told that Raj Kapoor's daughter wanted to meet him, not only did President Yeltsin agree to it, but he also wrote a note in his book. The note read, "I loved your father. He is still alive in our memories." These are just a few examples of Raj Kapoor's international popularity and the Hinduja brothers had contributed immensely to his international popularity, but they have never taken the credit for it.

Ranjeeta Ganeshan published an article titled 'Hindibaazi in Iran' in Business Standard (7 December 2019) wherein she mentioned in detail that Hindi cinema was very popular in Iranduring the sixties. She has also written extensively about the 'cinema friendship' between the Iranians and the Hindi cinema. Iranian writer and filmmaker Ehsan Khoshbakht, based in London, has written in the famous film magazine 'Sight and Sound' that Raj Kapoor had an important place in the cinema friendship of Iranians with Hindi cinema. The technology of cinema was not very developed 65-66 years ago today. Looking at Raj Kapoor's films, it appears that many times more impressive than the 'real sequences' are the images that we create in our minds. Today, it may seem strange to think that cinematic melodrama from India in Iran outclassed American and British cinema in the 1950s and beyond. This contribution of the Hinduja brothers to Hindi cinema is historic and has never been properly discussed in the media.

Raj Kapoor, Srichand Hinduja, Gopichand Hinduja, and others at the premiere of 'Shree 420' in Iran

Ranjita Ganesan writes that she came to know about the immense popularity of Hindi cinema in Iran during a visit to Iran in October-November 2019. There, a professor of film studies told her about the Persian word 'Hindibaazi' used to describe melodrama in Indian cinema. She also recounted how in those days it was often joked that 'tree' was an essential character in Hindi films around which the hero-heroine danced and sang. Hindi cinema was a great source of attraction as well as entertainment for Iranians. Such was the impact of these Hindi films that Indian characters were written in Iranian films and television serials. Most of the 'doctor' characters in the pre-revolution films were Indian as there were a large number of Indian doctors working in Iran at that time. In 1972, a film was made in Hindi and Persian, an Indo-Iranian co-production titled 'Subah-o-Sham,' which was named in Persian as 'Homay-e-Sadat'. Made in Iran, the Indian actress Waheeda Rehman played the role of a dancer in this film while Sanjeev Kumar and Iranian actor Fardeen played the roles of two real brothers. The film did well in Iran but didn't fare as per the expectations in India. The last co-production betweenIran and India was Murli Chhabria's 2016 film 'Salaam Mumbai,' starring Iranian superstar Raza Gulzar and Indian actress Dia Mirza as medical students in Mumbai. This film was a super hit in Iran, but it did not get any special attention in India.

The Hinduja brothers had screened G. P. Sippy and Ramesh Sippy's blockbuster film 'Sholay' in Iran, Turkey, and many other countries. Iran's state broadcasting organization 'Islamic Republic of Iran Broadcasting' (IRIB) conducted a survey in 2006 in which the Iranians rated the Hindi film 'Sholay' as the most favourite film. The censored copy of 'Sholay' is shown from time to time on Iran's state television channel IRIB. Owing to the large scale in which the Hinduja brothers screened Hindi films in Turkey at that time, there is still a demand for Hindi

cinema there. Gem TV, a television company operating illegally in Turkey, runs a popular channel of Hindi cinema called 'Gem Bollywood'.

The escapist nature of Hindi cinema made in Mumbai attracts the Afghans in Iran as well as the youth from those other countries that are witnessing civil war because it allows them to forget their grief and struggle at least for three hours. In this way, Hindi cinema serves as a stress buster for a large group of people. Youngsters are happy to imagine themselves in place of the heroes and heroines while watching Hindi movies. The Hinduja brothers may not know that this 'Hindibaazi' is proving to be of great use even for the youth who write scripts for popular cinema and television serials in Iran.

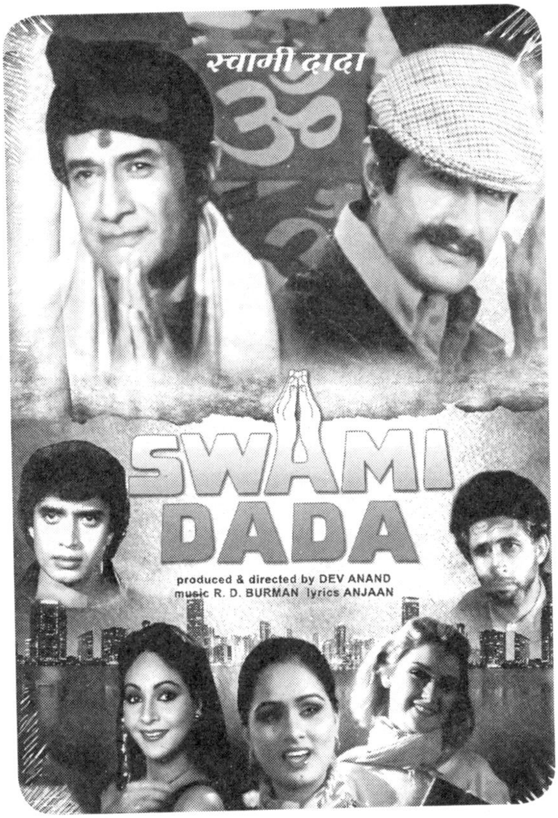
स्वामी दादा
SWAMI
DADA
produced & directed by DEV ANAND
music R. D. BURMAN lyrics ANJAAN

BETAAB

5

How the Hinduja Brothers Rescued the Indian Film Industry from the Economic Slowdown

Arvind Kumar had written many such editorials in the then famous cinema magazine 'Madhuri' of The Times of India Group, which show that the Indian film industry was going through a terrible financial crisis at that time. In the editorial published in the 7 May, 1965 issue of 'Madhuri,' he writes—

"A thick, dark cloud of crisis is looming over the film industry. Severe storms accompanied by torrential rains are knocking at the door. The film industry is not prepared to battle such a storm and so the situation is extremely delicate."

"For the past few months, the sources of credit to filmmakers have been fast drying up. Due to an acute shortage of money, they are finding it very difficult to complete their unfinished films. Studios often appear empty, and the work has been reduced to half. According to government documents, more than three hundred films are left incomplete in Bombay alone. In this budget, the government did not provideany relief to the film industry. On the contrary, the taxes on the import of raw film stock have been increased. The film producers were already upset about the levy imposed by the government. The government needs to reconsider its cinema-related economic policies."

The Hinduja brothers brought the Indian film industry out of recession during this period (in the 1960s and 1970s). Their financial help made sure that hundreds of films that were left unfinished due to a shortage of money got completed. At that time, there was no National Film Development Corporation (NFDC) or any financial company. And the banks did not give loans to filmmakers out of fear of losing money. Hinduja brothers invested money in all the major film production companies of that era and infused new life into them. But they did not take any credit and didn't even allow their names or the name of their company to be put in the film credits. The biggest example of this is GP Sippy's film 'Brahmachari,' which was stopped midway due to a lack of money. It was directed by Bhappi Soni and the lead roles were played by Shammi Kapoor, Mumtaz, and Pran. How the Hinduja brothers provided financial help to Raj Kapoor to make 'Bobby' after the debacle of 'Mera Naam Joker' has already been discussed. Similarly, the Hinduja brothers injected money into Manmohan Desai's film 'Coolie'. During the shooting of the film, Amitabh Bachchan had a life-threatening accident when an action sequence between him and Puneet Issar went out of control and Bachchan was left struggling for his life for many days. The entire country got together to pray for him, and the superstar eventually recovered. Khushal Chhabria of the Hinduja family also donated blood to Amitabh Bachchan at the Breach Candy Hospital. Apart from helping Manoj Kumar and Raj Kapoor, the Hindujas also injected money into Dev Anand's Navketan Films and Yash Johar's Dharma Productions.

Ashok Hinduja and Amitabh Bachchan

It is also surprising to see that whenever the Indian government was trying to promote Indian cinema abroad, between 1960 and 1970, there were failures due to various reasons. On the other hand, the Hinduja group tasted tremendous successes wherever they went. At that time there was a severe shortage of foreign capital in India. Due to this worldwide business of cinema, the Indian government was getting a huge amount of foreign capital—the record of which should be with the Reserve Bank of India and the Ministry of Information and Broadcasting, Government of India

Arvind Kumar had written many such editorials in 'Madhuri' magazine, which show that the Indian government was not serious about cinema and all its efforts were in vain. In an editorial published in the October 9, 1964 issue of 'Madhuri' titled 'Export of Indian Films,' he writes, "It is a matter of pleasure that the capital of Indian Motion Pictures Export Corporation Ltd. is being increased from ten lakh rupees to twenty five lakh rupees. This corporation will buy Indian films and commercialize them in foreign countries. In this way, the film industry will also be helpful in earning more foreign capital. Indian films have been helping to earn foreign capital in the past too. They were shown in areas where there are settlements of NRIs. There is also a need for our films to bewatched by the non-Indian audiences also."

No one knows what happened to this government body. How successful was it? Both the objectives mentioned in this editorial were accomplished by the Hinduja Group without any government support. They not only bought and exported about twelve hundred Hindi films abroad and earned a huge amount of foreign capital for the country, but also took our films to the non-Indian audiences.

In an editorial published in the December 17, 1965 issue of 'Madhuri' magazine titled 'Film Exports, Indian Style,' Arvind Kumar writes, "Officers of the Ministry of Information and Broadcasting of the Government of India and the Ministry of Culture of the Government of Egypt on 15 November 1965 are waiting at the Cairo International Airport to welcome a plane arriving from Bombay. Many eminent personalities from the Indian film industry are on that plane. A festival of Indian films is being held in Cairo wherein many Indian films are to be screened including 'Kashmir Ki Kali,' 'Woh Kaun Thi,' 'Hum Dono,' 'Sangam,' etc. The success of this film festival can open a huge market for Indian films in Egypt. This can give India an opportunity to earn a huge amount of foreign capital. This ceremony is taking place in a country that is our biggest Arab friend and is walking shoulder to shoulder with us in international politics. Among those coming from Bombay are Dev Anand, B.R. Chopra, Mala Sinha, Sadhna, etc. The plane arrives. The hosts move forward. What? None of the guests have come nor will come. The officers of the Indian embassy are buried in embarassment. Why they were not informed earlier about their absence? Now, what about the splendid banquets that were arranged in the honor of those who didn't show up? This style of functioning and red-tapism of our ministry is also well known in foreign countries".

"Now listen to the reason why none of the guests reached Cairo. B.R. Chopra had long ago told the officials of the Ministry of Information and Broadcasting that he would not go if his wife was not allowed to accompany him. He said that the

government allows other filmmakers to not only bring their wives but also their children to join the delegation. If the government did not want to give them this facility, then it should have arranged for some other representative or shouldn't have spread the false news of their coming to Cairo'.

"Similarly, Sadhna and Mala Sinha were also not ready to go alone. They wanted a member of their family to accompany them as their aide. The government officials were silent. It is said that three days before the film festival, the officers informed Sadhna that she could take only one person with her. By then she had given several dates for shooting in Bombay and her departure to Cairo would have cost the producers thousands of rupees, the responsibility of which would have been on her alone".

"Dev Anand was not a government representative earlier. He had refused to go to Cairo. He was in Rome on his way back from America on the opening day of the film festival and was boarding a plane to Bombay. He got the news from Delhi that he was now a government representative and had to go to Cairo. There was no clear information in this news piece that no other representative was reaching Cairo, so he must go there. Thinking that the rest would anyway reach Cairo, he returned to Bombay."

Ashok Hinduja and Amitabh Bachchan

The Hinduja brothers, in collaboration with the same Egyptian government, not only released Raj Kapoor's film 'Sangam' in Cairo but also released many more films. At the premiere of these films, the film artists associated with them were called in many countries and they never had any such problem as Arvind Kumar has written in his editorial above. The fact of the matter is that the Hinduja brothers got immense success in showing Hindi films abroad, taking our films to non-Indian audiences, creating a market for Indian films abroad, and earning foreign capital, and where the Indian government failed in these very objectives.

The Indian government once even tried to find a market for Indian films in America as well around the same period and failed again. In his editorial published in Madhuri's 18 December 1964 issue, Arvind Kumar writes— "A delegation was recently sent to America from the Film Export Development Corporation. The delegation also had taken some Indian films to America. The delegation's mission was: To examine the commercial potential of Indian films in America and find avenues for their promotion. What happened in America to the films screened by the delegation in America is now known to all. Nothing could have happened other than what actually happened there. Briefly and in polite words, the film businessmen and journalists there did not like our films".

"We have written in 'Madhuri' earlier also that the kind of films that are being made in our country these days cannot be exported".

It is to be noted here that the Hinduja brothers have successfully exported around twelve hundred similar films across the world and none of the films have suffered losses. I went through old issues of many important cinema magazines like 'Madhuri,' 'Filmfare,' and 'Screen' but could not find any material about the Hinduja brothers. The reason is clear. The Hinduja family did not want to promote or advertise itself. If they wanted, these magazines would have been full of articles and editorials about them.

Ashok Hinduja, Praful Patel, Sanjay Dutt with Gopichand Hinduja's daughter Ritu Chhabria

Arvind Kumar further writes—"We imitate Hollywood, just hollow imitation. We know how to set up grand sets. Even in photography, we are not far behind. We do a lot with whatever goods and furniture that we get. We offer dance and songs a little more than Hollywood. The audience finds everything in our movies. Seeing all this, our producers just cannot understand why our films are not liked in America. The trouble is that our films are unable to tie everything together in a way that the audiences find entertaining.

"Why should an American simply believe that a girl loves one young man but marries another? This seemingly simple thing will only be embraced by a foreigner when our films are so rich in Indianness that they are able to make a total stranger appreciate India and its values.

"This is why Satyajit Ray has been such a successful film director abroad, and perhaps he is the only Indian to represent our film industry there."

The Hinduja brothers did not create a world market for any art or parallel cinema. They created a world market for mainstream Hindi cinema. Here too, when the Indian government failed, the Hinduja brothers were always successful.

Ashok Parmanand Hinduja, the youngest brother of the Hinduja brothers, lives in Mumbai. He was born in 1950. Just last year he celebrated his 72nd birthday. Ashok Hinduja says, "Our childhood was spent in a simple way. When we grew up, we used to work three shifts. First, we used to go to college from 6.45-9.45 in the morning. After that, we used to help our father in his office. In the evening, at the office located on Charni Road, we used to handle the cinema business. We created an international market for Indian films. We gave jobs to hundreds of people. For example, Mohan Chhabria was sent to Israel. His elder brother Govardhan Chhabria was sent to Thailand and Govind Ram to Turkey. This is true that many people could not return our money so we would waive off their loans.You ask Jackie Shroff's wife Ayesha Shroff, and she will tell you how she suffered a huge loss with her film 'Boom' (2003) and she could not return our money. We simply wrote it off. In the last two films my daughter Ambika Hinduja invested in, 'Being Cyrus' (2006, Homi Adajania) and 'Teen Patti' (2010, Leena Yadav), we suffered huge losses with one of them. 'Teen Patti' had stalwarts like Amitabh Bachchan and Ben Kingsley and yet we suffered huge losses." Prakash Hinduja recalls the times when Mrs. Indira Gandhi was the Prime Minister of India, and American films were banned in India. With great difficulty she allowed the Hinduja brothers to import about 25 Hollywood films. Those films were dubbed in Hindi here in Bombay. The Hinduja brothers tried to tell Indian filmmakers through those films how good cinema is made. These films were then released in theaters across the country.

Prakash Hinduja often remembers his office at Charni Road in Mumbai and his dubbing center at Filmistan Studio. At that time he was only 17 years old.

G P Sippy's 'Brahmachari' was dubbed in the Thai language and was taken to Bangkok. Some South Indian films were also dubbed at the Filmistan Studios in Persian and screened in Iran.

Prakash Hinduja remembers one thing very clearly that when he got married in 1967, Hema Malini danced at his wedding party.

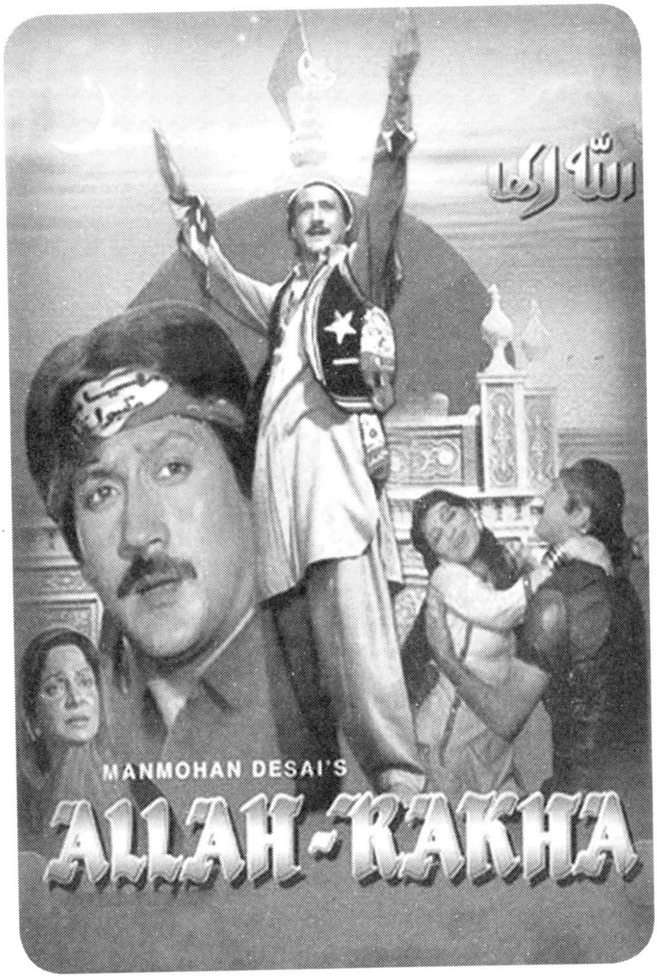

6

When the audience used to offer Namaz during the screening of this film in cinema halls

Fardeen Ali Ahmed, a daredevil filmmaker from Iran, went to Mecca-Medina to perform Haj with a video camera hidden in his clothes and hecaptured all the Haj rituals on that camera. After returning to Iran, he made a very good documentary. The Hinduja brothers bought it and screened it on a large scale in India. Its premiere in Delhi was attended by the then President of India, Dr. Zakir Hussain (1967-69). Prakash Hinduja says that the famous actor of his time, Kader Khan lent his voice for it and did the voice-over. The title of that film in Persian was – 'Khane Khuda' (1968) and in English, it was titled 'Pilgrimage to Mecca'. When this film was screened in the cinema halls of India, the Muslim audience started offering Namaz in the middle of the film only. At that time most of the Muslims of India could not go to the Haj pilgrimage due to poverty. For the first time, they were watching the Haj pilgrimage unfold on the cinema screen. Their holiest sites, Mecca and Medina, were right in front of them. Muslims all over the country came to see the film in huge numbers. This was the first time in the history of cinema that Mecca and Medina, the holiest sites of the Muslims, were filmed with great respect and reverence. The Hinduja brothers donated all the proceeds from this film to Muslim charities and in return, they were only happy to receive blessings from Muslims all across the country.

Cinema halls in Iran were named mostly after famous poets and writers there, such as 'Saadi,' 'Hafiz,' 'Moulin Rouge,' 'Homa,' 'Aasiya,' 'Firdous,' 'Khayyam,' 'Abdoh,' etc. During the Islamic Revolution, on 19 August, 1978, at eight o'clock in the night, radical Muslims set the 'Rex' cinema in the city of Abadan, Iran on fire and more than four hundred and twenty people were burnt to death. This was a sad event in the history of Iran's film industry, which the cinema lovers there still shudder to remember. It was in a way the beginning of the Islamic revolution in Iran. After this incident, the business of Hindi cinema in Iran almost came to an end. The Hinduja brothers had already sensed the changing tides and hadshifted the headquarters of their business from Tehran to London well before the start of the Islamic Revolution.

9891Murli Chhabria has been doing business in Iran for the last fifty years. He had handled the film business of Hinduja brothers in Iran and other countries for a long time. He says, "G.P. Sippy's blockbuster film 'Sholay' ran for a year in Tehran's 'Aasiya Theater'. G.P. Sippy himself went to Iran for its premiere. It was

Prakash Hinduja with Anupam Kher

at the Iran Studio in Tehran's Firdous Avenue where we would dub the Hindi films into Persian overnight. It was owned by Rajai. We used to bring Iranian artists whose voices were similar to the Indian film stars such as Raj Kapoor, Nargis, Waheeda Rehman, Vyjayanthimala, Dev Anand, Dilip Kumar, Manoj Kumar, Raj Kumar, and so on.Our system of dubbing films was very unique. It used to provide employment to Iranian artists. We used to edit 18 to 20 reels long Hindi films to 10 to 12 reels long films i.e. about two hours. The Hindi songs weren't dubbed into Persian and were shown with Persian subtitles. Since most of the songs of that era were in Urdu, the Persian and Arabic audiences didn't have much difficulty in understanding as many words in the Urdu language are similar to words in Arabic and Persian.

"Raj Kapoor's 'Sangam' created history in foreign countries and broke many records. Dev Anand's 'Guide' (1965) and 'Amir Garib' (1974) did well in Home Theatre. Manoj Kumar's 'Roti, Kapda Aur Makaan' (1974) and Firoz Khan's 'Dharmatma' (1975) and 'Qurbani' (1980) also did well in Home Theatre. We also had many other associates with us as well among whom Amarlal Hinduja, Kanhaiyalal, Narayan Das, Bhagwan Das, Nandlal, Chandulal, etc. were prominent.

There were also Ranchod Jumani and Ramesh Neechani who were relatives of the Hinduja family. Aasiya Films was registered in Bombay. There was also Rama Co-Enterprises Company. A new film was released every Wednesday in Iran. There were eight shows every day in Iran. At that time, when the minimum ticket for watching a movie in a cinema hall in India was two rupees, in Iran it was ten rupees. For the rich, there used to be a 'box' class in the cinema hall, which was called 'Lodge-e-Makhsoos,' whose ticket was fifty rupees. VIP visitors were served snacks consisting of Coca-Colaalong with pork, chicken, beetroot, and a variety of sandwiches. In those days there were only single-screen theaters in Iran. After the Islamic Revolution of 1979, the screening of Indian films in Iran drastically declined."

Prakash Hinduja with Amitabh Bachchan

"Indian films had a tremendous influence in those days, from the West Indies to the Far East and the Middle East countries. The Hinduja brothers opened their office at 29, Museum Street, WC 1, London under the name 'Sangam Limited'. Gopichand Hinduja has already told us about the success of our film 'Sangam' in London. The film had a grêat run at the Himalaya Theater in South Hall, London. Gulu Lalwani and Mehtani also used to work for us. We also went to Lebanon, Jordan, and Israel. There was a company called Handsome Limited Company in Tel Aviv, the capital of Israel. Mohamed Tahir was our agent in Jordan."

"There were about two thousand Hindus and Sikhs in Iran at that time. Before the release of a new film, Gopichand Hinduja used to organize a private evening show for free for the Indian people there and diplomats during which the entire film was shown without any cuts. About two hundred invited guests were alsoserved tea and snacks during the interval. Often this event was held at the Ice Palace Club. The first Indo-Iranian co-production was the 1972 film 'Subho Sham' (titled 'Humaye Shadat' in Persian) directed by Tapi Chanakya. In this film, theIndian actor Sanjeev Kumar played the part of Nasir alongside the Iranian actor Fardeen while Waheeda Rehman essayed the character of Sheereen, a dancer. It was a love story. The film did well in Iran and earned about two crore rupees. At that time our Hindi films in Iran used to do business of around seventy to eighty lakh rupees. The business formula in Iran was that 60 percent of the total earnings went to the owner of the cinema hall and 40 percent went to the Hinduja brothers. The cheapest ticket was Rs.10 with a profit of at least Rs.4 per seat. Films with social messages used to play a lot in Iran. Nargis starrer 'Mother India' (1957), Raj Kapoor starrer 'Boot Polish' (1954), and Raj Kumar starrer 'Paigham' (1959) did really well. We also released Amitabh Bachchan starrer 'Deewar' (1975) and Zanjeer' (1973). 'Paigham' acknowledged the power of the working class whereas 'Deewar' gave the message that bad deeds always result in bad consequences. Pramod Chakraborty's 'Dream Girl,' Pachhi's 'Around the World in Eight Dollars,' and 'Hit Run' also did well in Iran. The specialty of the Hinduja brothers was that they did everything legally. We always got permission certificates from the government. In Iran, we used to play Hindi films in about seventy theatres. Apart from Tehran, Hindi films also used to do a lot of business in the theaters of other cities of Iran like Mashad, Tabrish,

Isfahan, Janjan Awaaz, Abadan, Khurram, etc. The Shah of Iran used to watch Hindi movies in his palace. When the Hinduja brothers released Raj Kapoor's 'Jis Desh Mein Ganga Behti Hai' in Iran, Raj Kapoor came in the same costume that he wore in the film. Rajesh Khanna's film 'Hathi Mere Saathi' (1971) went housefull for six weeks in Iran. There used to be no elephants in Iran. But, the message of this film was very much liked by the Iranian people that one should not be cruel to animals and that animals can also be good friends of human beings. Rajesh Khanna was to come to Tehran but had to cancel at the last minute because he had a fever. Rajshri Production's film 'Dosti' (1964) also did well due to its message. In the first three days itself, there was a collection of nine thousand pounds. Taking the cost of three thousand pounds out, there was a net profit of six thousand pounds. Produced by B.R. Chopra and directed by his brother Yash Chopra 'Waqt' (1965) and 'Aadmi Aur Insaan' (1969) as well as 'The Train' (1970), starring Rajesh Khanna, ran successfully. Dharmendra—Hema Malini's 'Sita Aur Geeta,' Dilip Kumar's 'Ram Aur Shyam,' Manoj Kumar's 'Shor' and 'Purab Aur Paschim,' Dev Anand's 'Jewel Thief' and 'Guide,' Dharmendra's 'Jheel Ke Us Paar,' Dil Ek Mandir,' 'Khilona,' 'Suraj,' 'Dhool Ka Phool,' 'Mere Mehboob,' etc. were all well received by the Iranian audience".

"There was Ramnord Laboratory in Tardeo, Mumbai from where we used to get the negative prints made. From foreign agents, we used to take money in US dollars or British pounds. The office of Aasiya Corporation was situated on Charni Road. It was handled by the gentleman whose name was Girdhar Hinduja, but he was not one of the Hinduja brothers. C.K. Sundar used to look after the accounts and Ramesh Sheth looked after the public relations and publicity. We used to export films on the basis ofone print with two trailers and two prints with four trailers. R. K. Das, R. M. Shah, and Khushal Chhabria also worked with us. The Hinduja brothers financed hundreds of films, and invested money in them but did not take credit for any of them. From Raj Kapoor to Manoj Kumar and Manmohan Desai, the names of each of the films can actually be counted."

The son of the Hinduja brothers' sister, Sanjay Jumani, has seen this business of films very closely. He has a plethora of stories from that era to share. He recounts—"That era was something very different. Now when we remember that periodwe cannot believe that once there was such a big business of Hindi cinema all over the world. In that era, the Hinduja brothers exported all those films which can be described as superhits. V Shantaram's 'Dr Kotnis Ki Amar Kahani' and 'Do Aankhen Barah Haath,' Shammi Kapoor's 'Junglee,' 'Pagla Kahin Ka,' and 'Jawaan Mohabbat,' Manoj Kumar's 'Upkar,' 'Yadgaar,' and 'Kranti,' Amitabh Bachchan's 'Mard,' 'Coolie,' 'Dostana,' 'Naseeb,' 'Suhaag,' 'Toofan,' and 'Immaan Dharam,' Dharmendra's 'Naya Zamana,' and 'Jugnu,' Rajesh Khanna's 'Master Ji,' Pramod Chakraborty's 'Barood,' Kumar Gaurav-Rati Agnihotri starrer 'Ek Se Bhale Do.' The list is endless. We really created history".

Gopichand Hinduja and Prakash Hinduja

Prakash Parmanand Hinduja, Chairman (Europe) of Hinduja Group says, "I got married in Mumbai in 1967 and I remember Hema Malini danced at my wedding. At the time her first Hindi film 'Sapne Ka Saudagar' had not been released. All the important people in the film industry were present at the wedding. It was the biggest wedding of that era. All the important actors of the Bombay film industry, including Raj Kapoor, Dev Anand, Dilip Kumar, Raj Kumar, Manoj Kumar as well as film directors, film financiers, film producers, and film distributors attended. The wedding ceremony was held at the Turf Club, Race Course, Worli, Bombay. Immediately after the wedding, we went abroad for our honeymoon. First, we went to Jordan, then to Egypt, and finally to

Turkey. The biggest figure in the film business in Turkey was Limi Apecchi, who mainly distributed American films. When I went to make him a partner in the film business, he laughed seeing my young age. I was only twenty-three years old then. I did not mind his words and acted patiently. My wife said in a complaining tone,"We have come here on our honeymoon, and you have got busy doing business here too." I said, "Darling, while we are here, why not utilize this opportunity to make some money as well which can come in really handy during our honeymoon?"And I succeeded in making Limi Apecchi a partner in my company. We started with Raj Kapoor's 'Sangam' and later moved to 'Awaara'. After that, we released Ramanand Sagar's 'Arzoo,' which also had a great run. After this, there was a boom of Indian films in Turkey. Not only this, the Bombay filmmakers got their writers to write the stories keeping the Turkish films in mind".

"About a year after my marriage, I went to Bangkok, the capital of Thailand in 1968. On reaching Bangkok I first learned their local language 'Thai'. The dubbing system in Thailand was amazing. The dubbing did not take place in the studio. There used to be live dubbing when the picture was being played in the cinema hall. A girl and a boy used to sit in the projection room of the cinema hall. For all the female voices in the film, such as those of the wife, mother, girlfriend, female friend, maid, etc., a single girl used to speak their dialogues in the Thai language live. The girl didn't just read the dialogues, she would voice modulate them with the right feeling and emotions. Similarly, the boy used to take care of all the male voices in the film, such as those the hero, his father, friend, servant, and all the male characters. Both these artists had amazing preparation and practice. They were equally skilled when it came to films from America and other countries. While the film was being played, only the original dialogue was muted, and the sound score and background music continued. I had taken G. P. Sippy's film 'Brahmachari' to Thailand and had called Shammi Kapoor there for its premiere".

“I established Indian cinema in Beirut, Jordan, Syria, and Egypt as well. The business picked up. Then we went to Greece. There was a Hindi film there long ago and it was successful, but that relationship had got broken. So we released Raj Kapoor's ‘Sangam’ there and it became a super hit. After that, Hindi films became a rage in Greece. Our agent there was Demeskino Mekeldist.”

“I have already told you that when we released ‘Pilgrim to Mecca’ in India, our Muslim brothers and sisters started praying in the cinema hall itself. This film was distributed by Mecca Film Company. Our film company then brought it to India.”

The Hinduja Group's co-chairman Gopichand Hinduja says “In Iran, we used to often host feasts at our homes. But we served only vegetarian food. The Shah of Iran also used to come for them. He also used to eat vegetarian food only. I only used to ask my guests if they were allergic to any food item. Rest, I used to decide what I would serve them. When the President of India Dr. Radhakrishnan came to Iran, a banquet was organized in his honor at the Shah's palace. The food for it came from my house. Food for the Prime Minister of India, Morarji Desai too used to come from my house when he visited Iran.”

“There used to be a cinema hall called ‘Escala’ at the Totram Court Road area of London. When we told the manager of ‘Escala’ about the success story of ‘Sangam’ in Iran, Egypt, and all over the world and asked him to screen the film, the white man didn't believe us. He said that he could release ‘Sangam’ for two weeks if we bought the tickets of all the four shows on a huge commission. And so we did as he asked. ‘Sangam’ went Housefull in London too. Since then, the Hindi films started running in all four shows in London. We also helped a lot in the shooting of Manoj Kumar's film ‘Purab Aur Paschim’ in London”.

"We had also talked to Richard Attenborough to make a film on Mahatma Gandhi. Actually, Richard Attenborough had wanted to make a film on Mahatma Gandhi for a long time. That's when the Indian Government came to know about it. At the same time, the Government of India had created the National Film Development Corporation (NFDC). The government told us that since it was a matter of the Father of the Nation, Mahatma Gandhi, and the prestige of the country was attached to it, so the Indian Government should be allowed to produce the film. Hence, we backed out".

"We invested capital in hundreds of films from 1955 to 1978 when there was no NFDC and the banks did not give loans to filmmakers and our film industry was suffering from a terrible recession. We gave financial assistance to all the major filmmakers of that time".

"We are often asked why we left the film business. There were two reasons for this. One, our business had grown so much that we did not have time. Second, gradually some different types of people had started entering the film business for whom earning money was the only thing that mattered and by any means possible. People like Raj Kapoor, Dev Anand, Dilip Kumar had become rare. We sold our entire business related to cinema in 1978. However, even later on, we continued to help many filmmakers'.

"I had to move to Iran at the age of eighteen. It was 1958. There I realized the local language Persian dominated every sphere of life. I learned Persian within three weeks. There is a Gurudwara in Tehran of which I am still a trustee. I took every Prime Minister and the Leader of Opposition to Hare Krishna Temple (ISKCON) in London. John Major also went there and Michael Jackson too. Once there was a notice to close down the temple. I helped in every way possible to save the temple from closing down. The road behind the temple is named Dharam Marg after the late son of Srichand Hinduja, Dharam Hinduja.

"I keep on remembering the song from V. Shantaram's film 'Do Aankhen Barah Haath'—Ae Malik Tere Bande Hum. Our family is the first family that took Indian films all across the globe. The reason behind this was bigger than business because our films used to be colored in the colors of Indian culture. We were promoting Indianness and Indian culture across the world through our films. Today, our business is spread in more than a hundred countries of the world; we have offices in about 48 countries. But we never forget and as our father Parmanand Deepchand Hinduja used to say, 'Work to give'. Happiness comes from the blessings received."

7

And thus “Bollywood” Came to be–Gopichand Hinduja

What we call the golden Age of Hindi cinema was also the Golden Age of the global cultural journey of Hindi films. Today, Hindi films do good business across the world, butits foundation was laid in Iran in 1955 by the Hinduja brothers. This journey, which began in Iran, soon became popular all over the world. People today would find it hard to believe that about fifty years ago when Raj Kapoor's film 'Sangam,' dubbed in Persian, was released in Iran, it ran there for three years. It also ran for a whole year in Cairo, the capital of Egypt. Between 1955 and 1984, the Indian industrialists, the Hinduja brothers screened not only 'Sangam' but also another 1200 Hindi films across the world and that's how'Bollywood' came to be.Several interesting anecdotes from this glorious unwritten history of Hindi cinema have been revealed for the first time by industrialist Gopichand Hinduja, England's richest person of Indian origin, in his conversation with Ajit Rai. This conversation, between *Ajit Rai* and *Gopichand Hinduja,* took place in London over several meetings.Here are the key revelations. This conversation was first published in Navbharat Times, India's leading Hindi daily, simultaneously in the New Delhi, Mumbai and Lucknow editions along with all its online and international editions on Saturday, 30 January 2021.

> *Gopichand ji, the global cultural journey of Hindi cinema that started in Iran in 1955, how did the idea come about, after all, you had gone to Iran to do business?*

Trading is an art we have inherited from the five thousand year old Indus Valley Civilization; that was when we humans on earth got our first lessons in organized trade and banking. Steeped in this heritage, in 1914, my father Parmanand Deepchand Hinduja (1901–1971) left Shikarpur city in Sindh province, now in Pakistan, and came to Mumbai. In 1919, he left for Iran and set up an office in Tehran. He was the first Indian to establish a business office outside India. Later, when the business grew, my father sent for my eldest brother Girdhar Hinduja (1932–1992) to join him from Mumbai. At that time, a large number of Indians worked in Iran. This was a foreign country, with a culture different from ours; so Bhai Saheb (Girdhar Hinduja) thought of showing Hindi films here. This way, the Indians could be entertained and our culture would also get promoted simultaneously. Srichand Hinduja, my second elder brother who also lived in Mumbai at that time was entrusted with this work; our youngest brother Ashok Hinduja used to help him. Later Prakash Hinduja, my younger brother, took over the job. Karan Johar's company, Dharma Productions, is named after Srichand's son Dharam Hinduja. You know, Karan Johar's father, Yash Johar, had worked with us back then. Srichand was a friend of Raj Kapoor, so it all started in Iran with Raj Kapoor's film 'Shree 420'. The year was 1955. Our father, however, was not in favour of the cinema business. He made us promise that everything we would do would be above board; we did, and we have kept our word.

At that time, Hollywood films dominated the scene in Iran and alternatively, there were Iranian films that were being screened, how did you manage to establish Hindi cinema as big business?

Gopichand Hinduja Presenting Asha Bhonsle with a Lifetime Achievement Award for her Special Contribution to Cinema

There is a very interesting story. We took Raj Kapoor to Tehran in October 1964 to screen his film 'Sangam' at the classiest of all cinema halls: 'Saadi'. 'Sangam' had completed three housefull weeks in 'Saadi' but its owner was not at all happy.

He simply informed me that he was discontinuing the screenings as he felt that it would not go well with his Hollywood film viewing patrons,which, in turn, could badly affect his business. I spent a sleepless night wondering what would happen next. The next morning, I went to meet the owner of 'Hafiz,' the cinema hall right across 'Saadi'. A Hollywood film, 'Four Horses,' was being screened there. He told me that business was not doing well and the monetary position was tight. I gave him a loan of ten lakh rupees on the condition that he would screen our Hindi films in his cinema hall 'Hafiz'. He was overjoyed. That very day, he dropped the Hollywood film 'Four Horses' and started screening our film 'Sangam' for the 3 o'clock show. 'Sangam' went on to create a record there by running continuously for three years.Cinema halls in Tehran were named after famous Persian writers.

At that time the upper class in Tehran only went towatch Hollywood movies. Hollywood movies ran no more than four, five, or six days because there were onlyso many upper-class patrons. On the other hand, Hindi cinema connected with the general Iranian audience. Habib Malik, the owner of 'Shahbaz'cinema, was so madly in love with Hindi cinema that it always became a tough job to get him to take off a film after its run was over.

Were Hindi movies released in Iran with Persian or English subtitles?

Initially it was so, but later we started a dubbing office in Mumbai's Filmistan Studio where we would dub Hindi films into Persian. We used to call artists from Iran whose voices matched those of our Indian artists. Not only that, I used to edit the 18-20 reel movies down to 10-12 reels. People began to believe that I had mastered film editing.

I had cut 'Sangam' in Persian to make the four-hour film into a two-hour one without informing Raj Kapoor. My brother Srichand had brought Raj Kapoor to Teheran for its premiere, and I was quite worried about his reaction. At the

Prakash Hinduja, Shashi Kapoor, and Gopichand Hinduja

screening of the film that evening, we sat in the balcony, all three of us. Srichand and I sat on either side of Raj Kapoor. He watched the entire film quietly, gently sipping the Scotch, we had specially ordered for him from London. However, as soon as the film was over, he got up and hugged me. Complimenting me on the editing he said that even he could not have done a better job. That said, subsequently, he always showed me his films first and sought my opinion before he went ahead.

For the Iranian audiences, after a thorough dissection of each and every Hindi film, we in a way created a new version of the film. This often involved changing names and even dialogues. For example, the 1956 film 'Durgeshnandini' based on the novel of Bankim Chandra Chatterjee was released in Iran titled 'Farman-e-Akbar'. Similarly, Dev Anand's 'Guide' was renamed 'Rahnuma'. We released almost all the big films of that time in Iran.Inspired by our success in Iran, we released Hindi films in Jordan, Egypt, Lebanon, Syria, Greece, Thailand, and other countries.

How were Indian artists like Raj Kapoor, Nargis, Sunil Dutt, and Waheeda Rehman received in Iran at that time?

At the time Raj Kapoor's film 'Shree 420' (1955) was running quite well. We bought it for five thousand rupees with a minimum guarantee and released it in Iran with a Persian subtitles.

Caption 3: Gopichand Hinduja and Randhir Kapoor

The premiere of this film in Tehran also has its own tale to tell. With great difficulty Srichand Parmanand Hinduja had persuaded Raj Kapoor to come to Iran (Tehran). He fetched Raj Kapoor from his Sion office in his car and headed towards the airport. On the way, Raj Kapoor spoke of some problem that had arisen at his home due to which he could not go to Iran. Some controversy had arisen regarding Raj Kapoor's wife Krishna Kapoor and Nargis. This put everyone in a fix. All the arrangements for the premiere of the film has already been made in Iran. Somehow, Srichand managed to persuade Raj Kapoor to go to Tehran. Raj Kapoor had agreed only on the condition that Srichcand would drink Scotch with him on the plane all the way to Iran. Those days, there were no direct flights to Iran and onehad to change aircraft at Karachi. On his way to Karachi, Raj Kapoor had drunk so much that he needed support toget off the plane. Srichand was upset as a large crowd of Pakistanis had gathered to see Raj Kapoor at the Karachi Airport.The next morning, however, Raj Kapoor apologized to Srichand for his behaviour. A huge crowd gathered for the premiere of the film in Tehran's cinema hall 'Koochay Laalzaar'. Seeing Raj Kapoor come up on stage in a blue suit and red tie, the Iranians mistook him for a communist. After the show, however,

Raj Kapoor had become a superstar in Iran. He was mobbed by the thronging crowd. The police had to be called and he was rescued by being seated in the back of an armoured vehicle meant for transporting prisoners.

Gopichand Hinduja and actor Ali Fazal in London

'Shree 420' did very well in Iran. Incredible as it may seem today, it ran continuously for a year and a half at the 'Shahbaz' cinema in Tehran, raking in tremendous profits for the company. Raj Kapoor's first film 'Aag' (1948) was also released by us in Iran, but it was less successful. Dev Anand and Geeta Bali's 'Baazi' was not as successful. This process went on and we went on to screen about twelve hundred Hindi films in different countries outsideIndia and not a single film suffered a loss.All the big and successful films of that era were with us. Sunil Dutt and Nargis attended the premiere of 'Mother India' (1957) in Tehran. By then, Nargis was already a superstar in Iran whereas Sunil Dutt was not known at all. The Iranians were desperate to catch a glimpse of her. When they came together for the premiere, theIranians mobbed Nargis, totally ignoring Sunil Dutt who got very upset because of it. Girdhar ji then had to keep Sunil Dutt distracted with other things while the people had their fill of Nargis' superstardom.

How did you make Hindi cinema successful in London? Before 'Sangam' there was no Hindi film in all the four shows.

'Escala' was a cinema hall in Totram Court area of London. The manager at 'Escala' refused to believe us when we told him about the success of 'Sangam' in Iran, Egypt and other parts of the world and asked him to release the film. He was willing to release 'Sangam' for all four shows for two weeks if we agreed to buy all the tickets at a huge commission, which we did. 'Sangam' ran to full houses in London, too. Since then, Hindi films started appearing in all four shows in London.Earlier, in London, Hindi films were screened only on weekend matinee shows. We also helped Manoj Kumar a lot with the shooting of his film 'Purab Aur Paschim' in London.

You guys had talked to Richard Attenborough to make the film 'Gandhi,' what happened afterwards? Why did you leave this film?

Yes, we were in talks with Richard Attenborough but when the Indian Government came to know about it. By that time, the Government of India had already set up NFDC, the National Film Development Corporation. As the film was about Mahatma Gandhi, the Father of the Nation,and the prestige of the country was attached to it; it was felt that the Indian Government should be allowed to produce this film. That is why, we withdrew.

We invested capital in hundreds of films from 1955 to 1978 when there was no NFDC, banks did not give loans to filmmakers and our film industry was suffering from a terrible recession. We gave financial assistance to all the major filmmakers of that time.

Why did you bid adieu to the film business?

There were two reasons for this. First, our business had grown and needed more hands-on involvement. Second, people like Raj Kapoor, Dev Anand, and Dilip Kumar were not to be found in the film business, instead, a new lot was seen coming whose prime motivation was only money and making it in any whichever way possible. This was not our way. Hence, in 1978, we sold our entire cinema-related business to Lalchand Lund. Nonetheless, we did not disconnect completely and continued to help many filmmakers, even after that.

पराई संस्कृति थी, सोचा हिंदी फिल्में दिखाई जाएं

*जिसे हम हिंदी सिनेमा का स्वर्ण युग कहते हैं, वह हिंदी फिल्मों की वैश्विक सांस्कृतिक यात्रा का भी स्वर्ण युग था। हिंदी फिल्मों का बिजनेस आज सारी दुनिया में अच्छा चल रहा है, लेकिन इसकी बुनियाद 1955 में हिंदुजा बंधुओं ने ईरान में रखी थी। 1955 से 1984 तक करीब 1200 हिंदी फिल्मों को हिंदुजा बंधुओं ने दुनिया भर में प्रदर्शित किया, और इस तरह बना बॉलिवुड। हिंदी सिनेमा के इस गौरवशाली अलिखित इतिहास को लेकर इंग्लैंड में भारतीय मूल के सबसे अमीर इंसान, उद्योगपति गोपीचंद हिंदुजा ने **अजित राय** से बातचीत में कई दिलचस्प खुलासे किए। लंदन में हुई इस बातचीत के मुख्य अंश :*

सप्ताह का इंटरव्यू

गोपीचंद हिंदुजा

> तेहरान में उच्च वर्ग केवल हॉलिवुड की फिल्में देखने जाता था जो चार-पांच दिन में उतर जाती थीं क्योंकि उच्च वर्गीय दर्शकों की संख्या काफी कम थी। हिंदी सिनेमा ने आम ईरानी दर्शकों को जोड़ा। शाहबाज सिनेमा का मालिक हबीब मलिक हिंदी फिल्मो का दीवाना हो गया था। मुश्किल से फिल्म उतारने पर राजी होता

■ गोपीचंद जी, हिंदी सिनेमा की सांस्कृतिक वैश्विक यात्रा की जो शुरुआत 1955 में ईरान में हुई, इसका विचार कैसे आया क्योंकि आप लोग तो वहां व्यापार करने गए थे?

व्यापार कला तो हमें पांच हजार साल पुरानी सिंधु घाटी सभ्यता से विरासत में मिली है, जब इस धरती पर इंसान ने संगठित व्यापार और बैंकिंग का पहला पाठ पढ़ा था। मेरे पिता परमानंद दीपचंद हिंदुजा उसी विरासत को लेकर पाकिस्तान के सिंध प्रांत के शिकारपुर शहर से 1914 में मुंबई (तब बंबई) आए थे। वे 1919 में ईरान गए और तेहरान में अपना दफ्तर खोला। भारत से बाहर अपना बिजनेस ऑफिस खोलने वाले वे पहले भारतीय थे। बाद में बिजनेस चल निकला तो पिताजी ने मुंबई से मेरे सबसे बड़े भाई गिरिधर हिंदुजा को वहां बुला लिया। गिरिधर के बेटे धरम हिंदुजा के नाम पर ही करण जौहर की कंपनी है धर्मा प्रॉडक्शन। करण जौहर के पिता यश जौहर हमारे साथ काम कर चुके थे। उस समय ईरान में बड़ी संख्या में भारतीय काम करते थे। पराया देश था, पराई संस्कृति थी, तो भाई साहब ने सोचा कि क्यों न यहां हिंदी फिल्में दिखाई जाएं जिससे भारतीयों का मनोरंजन हो और हमारी संस्कृति का भी प्रचार-प्रसार हो। मेरे दूसरे बड़े भाई श्रीचंद हिंदुजा को मुंबई में इस काम में लगाया गया। वहां हमारे सबसे छोटे भाई अशोक हिंदुजा उनकी मदद करते थे। बाद में प्रकाश हिंदुजा ने यह काम संभाला, जो मुझसे छोटे भाई हैं। श्रीचंद राजकपूर के मित्र थे। तो यह सिलसिला ईरान में राजकपूर की फिल्म 'श्री 420' से 1955 में शुरू हुआ।

■ ईरान में तो उस समय हॉलिवुड की फिल्मों का बोलबाला था या फिर ईरानी फिल्में चलती थीं। फिर आप लोगों ने हिंदी सिनेमा का इतना जबरदस्त बिजनेस कैसे स्थापित किया?

इसकी भी बड़ी दिलचस्प कहानी है। हमने तेहरान के सबसे संभ्रांत सिनेमा हाल 'सादी' में राज कपूर को ले जाकर अक्टूबर 1964 में 'संगम' फिल्म लगाई जो तीन हफ्ते हाउसफुल गई। फिर 'सादी' का मालिक बदहवास मेरे पास आया और बोला कि उसने 'संगम' फिल्म उतार दी है क्योंकि हॉलिवुड की फिल्में देखने के अभ्यस्त उसके संभ्रांत दर्शक नाराज हो जाएंगे और उसका बिजनेस चौपट हो जाएगा। दूसरी सुबह मैं ठीक उसके सामने के सिनेमा हाल 'हाफिज' के मालिक से मिलने गया। उसने कहा कि पैसे की बड़ी तंगी है, बिजनेस ठीक नहीं चल रहा। मैंने उसे इस शर्त पर दस लाख रुपए का कर्ज दिया कि वह हाफिज सिनेमा हॉल में हमारी हिंदी फिल्में लगाएगा। वह खुशी से उछल पड़ा। उसी दिन शाम तीन बजे के शो में उसने हॉलिवुड की 'फोर हॉर्सेज' उतारकर हमारी 'संगम' लगा दी। फिर तो 'संगम' ने रिकार्ड तोड़ दिया और तीन साल चली। उस जमाने मे तेहरान में उच्च वर्ग केवल हॉलिवुड की फिल्में देखने जाता था जो चार-पांच दिन में उतर जाती थीं क्योंकि उच्च वर्गीय दर्शकों की संख्या काफी कम थी। हिंदी सिनेमा ने आम ईरानी दर्शकों को जोड़ा। शाहबाज सिनेमा का मालिक हबीब मलिक हिंदी सिनेमा का दीवाना हो गया था। बड़ी मुश्किल से वह फिल्म उतारने पर राजी होता।

■ क्या ईरान में हिंदी फिल्में फारसी या अंग्रेजी सबटाइटल्स के साथ रिलीज होती थीं?

शुरू में ऐसा था, पर बाद में हमने मुंबई के फिल्मिस्तान स्टूडियो में एक डबिंग ऑफिस खोला जिसमें सारी हिंदी फिल्मों को हम फारसी में डब कर देते थे। हम ईरान से वैसे कलाकारों को बुलाते थे जिनकी आवाजें भारतीय कलाकारों से मिलती जुलती थीं। इतना ही नहीं, मैं 18-20 रील की फिल्मों को संपादित करके 10-12 रील की बना देता था। लोगों का मानना था कि मुझे फिल्म एडिटिंग में महारत हासिल है। मैंने राज कपूर से बिना बताए फारसी में 'संगम' को काटकर चार घंटे से दो घंटे की फिल्म बना दी। तेहरान में उसके प्रीमियर पर श्रीचंद हिंदुजा राज कपूर को लेकर आए। मैं अंदर से डरा हुआ था कि कहीं वे नाराज न हो जाएं। शाम को फिल्म का प्रीमियर शुरू हुआ। थियेटर की बालकनी में राज कपूर के एक ओर श्रीचंद बैठे और दूसरी ओर मैं। जब तक फिल्म चलती रही, राज कपूर चुपचाप फिल्म देखते रहे और स्कॉच पीते रहे जो हमने उनके लिए खासतौर पर लंदन से मंगवाई थी। फिल्म खत्म होने पर उन्होंने मुझे गले लगा लिया और कहा कि इतनी अच्छी एडिटिंग खुद वे भी नहीं कर सकते थे। उसके बाद उन्होंने जो भी फिल्म बनाई, सबसे पहले मुझे दिखाई और मेरी सलाह ली।

■ आप लोग रिचर्ड एटनबरो से 'गांधी' फिल्म बनाने के लिए बात कर चुके थे, बाद में आपने यह फिल्म क्यों छोड़ दी?

हां, हम बात कर चुके थे। तभी भारत सरकार को इस बारे में पता चला। उसी समय भारत सरकार ने राष्ट्रीय फिल्म विकास निगम (एनएफडीसी) बनाया था। सरकार ने हमसे कहा कि यह राष्ट्रपिता महात्मा गांधी का मामला है और इससे देश की प्रतिष्ठा जुड़ी है इसलिए इस फिल्म को उसे ही प्रोड्यूस करने दिया जाए। इस वजह से हम बाहर आ गए।

■ आपने फिल्म बिजनेस को अलविदा क्यों कह दिया?

इसकी दो वजहें थी। एक तो हमारा बिजनेस इतना बढ़ गया था कि हमारे पास समय नही बचता था। दूसरे, धीरे-धीरे सिनेमा बिजनेस में कुछ अलग तरह के लोग आने लगे थे जिनके लिए किसी भी तरह पैसा कमाना ही मुख्य हो गया था।

Navbharat Times, 30 January, 2021

8

Har Dil Jo Pyaar Karega,
Woh Gaana Gaayega
(Every heart that reverberates
with love cannot help but sing)
—Gopichand Hinduja

Raj Kapoor's daughter Ritu Nanda has written a book on her father—'Raj Kapoor: The One and Only Showman.' The book was published in 2017 by HarperCollins Publishers. In this book, Gopichand Hinduja has written a commentary about Raj Kapoor which is printed on pages 240-244. Here with gratitude, we are giving an important comment written by Gopichand Hinduja from that book—**Ajit Rai**

In 1957, we started distributing Raj Kapoor's many masterpieces to the world audiences. At the many premieres we organized overseas, fans became ecstatic! This business association transformed into a close family relationship between us and Raj, Krishna-ji (the centre of his life), and his gifted children. This relationship with Raj Kapoor remains among our fondest memories. I salute those who put in their best without worrying about returns. "Har dil jo pyaar karega, woh gaana gayega" (Every heart that reverberates with love cannot help but sing). The above line says it all. Raj-ji was not just a great showman; he was the complete showman, a philosophical showman who understood the rare nuances of life and captured it in such a simple manner that it created an instantaneous bond with his audience. He was a good soul whose heart reverberated for the common man. A rare filmmaker—a producer to an actor to being a director to being its musician—all rolled into one; such consummate proficiency in the craft is extremely hard to come by. He built his team who understood his vision, uniquely backed him up, and read his mind perfectly to bring out on celluloid, exactly what he wanted. To this day, no one has been able to replace him and perhaps, no one ever will. He lived and breathed his films. They were his life's philosophy depicted on 70mm. His creations are timeless and therefore, he too remains a timeless creation of the Almighty.

As a person, he was the life of every occasion; be it a party, just an informal gathering, or a premiere. The relationship with the Hinduja family was built with his fondness for my late eldest brother, Girdhar Hinduja. It was then nurtured by my elder brother, Srichand, and me. Having distributed his films overseas, I can vividly recall many of the instances of the times spent with him, up close and about. In Russia and Middle Eastern markets including Iran, he was as popular as Prime Minister Nehru and in some countries, his popularity even soared past Nehru's.

Raj Kapoor at Srichand Hinduja's marriage ceremony alongside him and his father Parmanand Hinduja

Raj Kapoor was an excellent ambassador of Indian culture, abroad. Worldwide, whether it was Syria, Jordan, Greece or even London, it is a credit to Raj Kapoor only that Indian cinema could tap into overseas markets and pave the way for the Bollywood of today. Back then in London, Indian films used to run at most for a matinee show on weekends. When Sangam was released, we had booked the cinema halls in London for the entire week, much to the surprise of theatre owners who thought we had gone crazy. But when Sangam ran to a full house, show after show, it was Raj Kapoor and us, who had the last laugh.

At the Shri 420 premiere which was organized in Tehran, where he was invited, the whole lane leading up to the venue was so crowded with his fans that it became practically impossible for him to leave the venue. I remember, he had come wearing navy blue suit and sported a red tie. Now red was a colour that symbolized Communism, then and it was not a favoured ideology of the then Iranian regime. We made him remove his red tie, and arranged for the Iranian Police who slipped him out of the cinema hall through the back door, shoved him into a jailor's van, and sped off.

Raj Kapoor with Srichand Hinduja and an Iranian dubbing artist at Hinduja Brothers' film office

He was so popular with women that they used to queue up outside our home, whenever he came visiting, not to kiss him but to be kissed by him. In fact, one of our local Iranian friends used to joke with us that we should send all those waiting women to him so that he could screen which of them was fit enough to meet the "Great Raj Kapoor". Raj loved nightlife and nightclubs. Whenever he visited one, invariably the running show would be stopped, and he would be asked to take centre-stage and takeover. Never the one, to disappoint any, he would impromptu, break into his numbers from Awaara, Mera Naam Joker, Shri 420, etc. The claps would never stop egging him on and on... he always obliged because he and his fans were inseparable.

In Tehran, his magnum opus, 'Sangam,' ran for 3 years continuously and was houseful from the first to the last show!! One has often heard of a local language film having such record runs in one's own country. But for an Indian film to run for 3 years at a stretch, without break, in a foreign land like Iran, where the average run for any movie to date has not been more than 3 weeks—I am yet to come across one. Once he was invited to inaugurate a TV station in Iran. Not to be satisfied with ribbon cutting and button pressing, he landed up at the inauguration in the costume with dholak, etc. singing, "Hum us desh ke

vaasi hain, jis deshmein Ganga behti hai" (We are inhabitants of that country in which the sacred river the Ganges flows). The inauguration created waves. To this day, that TV station runs and continues to thrive. In Iran, the now-famous singer, Gogoosh, then only a child artist, built her career singing Ichak Daana Pichak Daana... with the help of Raj Kapoor.

The usual contract for overseas rights for films includes a clause that the film would not be edited. But to adapt to local market requirements, we had edited and dubbed 'Sangam' in Farsi. The movie had a Platinum Jubilee run!! Raj Kapoor came and insisted that he would like to see this version. We dissuaded him since he would have watched it many times. He insisted and we had to relent. Throughout the movie, I was virtually on my toes, afraid of his famous temper. To my surprise, he hugged me at the end of the film, commenting "Even I couldn't have edited it any better".

Music and songs stirred his soul. He used to take personal interest even in the lyrics and music of each and every song of his film.

He often used to come to London at our home, sit on the ground with a harmonium at hand, and sing. Once he sang "Jaane kahan gaye woh din" (Alas! Where have those days gone)—the signature song of his philosophical auto-biography, 'Mera Naam Joker,' which was then in works. Then he asked, "Gopi... Kya kehta hai?" (Gopi, what do you say?) I immediately told him – it would be a hit and hit, it was.

Raj had a great zest for life and was a great lover of food. When he used to throw private parties, he himself used to carefully choose the menu and what a wonderful host he was which added to the flavor of the lip-smacking dishes that used to be in the elaborate spread. He came to Tehran once; I had just got married then. It was 3 am in the morning and he gave me a call saying he wanted to eat Kalle Paache (special cooked Head and Feet of Lamb—an Iranian delicacy). Being a pure vegetarian and considering the odd hour, I took him to a restaurant opposite a nightclub. Seeing him relish his food with vodka, even the owner of the restaurant got bewildered and advised me to not serve him more. When he had had his fill, I took him and deposited him in his room at Hilton where he woke up well past

afternoon, the next day. He called me and said, let's go out somewhere to enjoy. Such was his appetite for life. Beating the bevy of waiting girls in the hotel lobby, with great difficulty, we shoved ourselves into a car and sped off to a ski resort at Aabe' Ali. His close friend and co-actor, Rajendra Kumar, was also with us. Three of us, rode on ponies, into the mountains and had a great time there. He confessed to me, "This was the best outing experience I have ever had so far".

Along with his elegant wife, Krishna, and three children, Randhir, Rishi, and Ritu, he came to the weddings of my brother SP and mine, which happened to be on the same day. To all the guests, he announced that "I am part of the Hinduja Family".

He borrowed the Gandhi cap that my father used to wear and sporting it, he posed it with all of us in our wedding photographs. After him, Krishna Bhabhi and her children have nurtured this long-standing family relationship with ours and even today it continues to thrive. When we moved to London, we named our London HQ on one of his master creations–'Sangam Limited'. Because he was family. He lives on in our hearts: our brother, Raj.

9

What Do People in the Film Industry Say?

If we look at the history of the Hindi film industry from 1954-55 to 1984-85, we find that during this period there was no major production house in Mumbai which did not work with the Hinduja brothers or whose films were not released by the Hinduja brothers abroad. Most of the films that we consider today as blockbusters, super-duper hits, and films of cultural and historical importance, the Hinduja brothers not only invested money in them but also released them worldwide. Here are the thoughts of some eminent personalities of the film industry on this topic—

Hinduja Brothers have been the Pillars of Strength in our Film Industry: Dharmendra

Legendary actor of Hindi cinema, Dharmendra, says, "Hinduja brothers have been the pillars of strength in our film industry on whose foundationsthe entire Bollywood of today has developed. I remember that in those days, the Hindi film industry was going through a terrible recession. Banks did not give loans to the people. Due to the paucity of money, many films used to stop being produced in the middle. At that time, the Hinduja brothers helped our film industry a lot. They were always willing to extend their help to those in need. Sunny Deol's first 'Betaab' (1983) was financed by the Hinduja brothers only. Even after that whenever I approached them, all my worries used to go away as soon as I spoke to them. They helped me with an open heart. I will not go into details. All I would say is that my family relationship with the Hinduja brothers, once formed, is intact till date".

Dharmendra recalls that the Hinduja brothers also helped a lot in the shooting of Ramanand Sagar's 'Ankhen'. He says, "I went to Iran on their invitation and they gave me tremendous love there, took care of me a lot. Ranchod Jumani used to accompany me in Tehran. Later, they openly supported almost all our films. They also took me to many other countries. I was surprised to see that our films were liked and well received there."

The Hinduja Brothers Named their Office in Tehran as Arzoo: Prem Sagar

Recalling that period, Ramanand Sagar's son Prem Sagar says, "When the Hinduja brothers released our film 'Arzoo' (1965) worldwide, it created a great buzz all around. The film was successful at the box office even in those countries where we could not have imagined it. The film went to all the five continents as well as to the South American countries. 'Arzoo' did good business in the Middle East, Suriname, and Peru. When the film was running in Malaysia, a boy and a girl used to do 'live manual dubbing' together from both sides of the screen. The soundtrack of the dialogues of the film's cast was turned off and the boy would voice modulate the dialogues for all the male characters and the girl would voice modulate the dialogues for all the female characters of the film in the Malay language. This was Prakash P. Hinduja's idea." Prem Sagar further says, "Parmanand Hinduja's global vision was very big. It was because of his vision that the Hinduja family has achieved so much. My father Ramanand Sagar knew Parmanand Hinduja since 1950 when the Hinduja brothers were very young. One of the specialties of these people was that they didn't just become business partners but they would also become family friends. And they would look after you so well. The Hinduja brothers are the most important contributor to the global success of the film 'Arzoo'. You have to understand that they opened cinema halls for Hindi films in many places like British Guiana, Jakarta (Indonesia), etc. Pradeep Santhani used to handle their work in British Guiana. Our film 'Arzoo' was so successful worldwide that the Hinduja brothers kept the telegraphic address of their office in Tehran as 'Arzoo'. In London, they named it as 'Sangam'".

Prem Sagar recalls, "When my father started the film 'Ankhen' (1968), it was to be shot in many countries of the world such as Japan, Venice (Italy), Hong Kong, Singapore, Beirut, etc. Had the Hinduja brothers not helped my father, the film could not have been made. Firstly, they had reliable people everywhere abroad, and, secondly, there was a terrible shortage of foreign capital in India in those days. Srichand Hinduja and Gopichand Hinduja were of great help in Tehran. There they took the film unit, which also had Dharmendra, to a restaurant that used to serve 'soda lassi' and delicious kebabs, and there were cots instead of chairs and tables for sitting.

"There was an office in Mumbai's Tardeo area called 'Film Center,' where people used to work all night long. It was here that dubbing and editing of films in Persian were done. It was owned by Shashi Bhai Patel, whose brother, Ramesh Patel's daughter married Ramesh Sippy. Speaking of marriage, I still remember that the music used in Ram and Sita's marriage in our serial 'Ramayana' was taken from the wedding of the Hinduja brothers. Whenever we went to London, we definitely went to the Hinduja brothers' house for savoring some vegetarian Sindhi food. Many times, we used to walk from Hay Market, where their office is today, to their home at Carlton House Terrace. As soon as we got there, we would be thrilled wondering that the house where the Hinduja family lived, and where we were eating, was once inhabited by Britain's Queen Victoria."

For the Hinduja Brothers, it was not the Money but the Intention that Mattered: Ketan Desai

Ketan Desai, son of famous filmmaker Manmohan Desai, says, "The Hinduja brothers supported all my father's films in one way or the other, starting from his early film 'Chhaliya' (1960, Raj Kapoor, Nutan, Pran, Rehman, etc.) to the last film 'Anmol' (1993, Rishi Kapoor, Manisha Koirala). But, at least, five of our films were completely made by them. Four of them were by my father Manmohan Desai: Naseeb (1981), Coolie (1983), Mard (1985), and Toofan (1989) while the last film Alla Rakha (1986, Jackie Shroff, Dimple Kapadia, Shammi Kapoor) was mine. Amitabh Bachchan played major roles in all these films of my father. Along with these films, Amar Akbar Anthony

(1977, Amitabh Bachchan, Vinod Khanna, Rishi Kapoor, Pran, Parveen Babi, Neetu Singh, Shabana Azmi), and Suhaag (1979) were also released by the Hinduja brothersall over the world. Their brother-in-law Khushal Chhabria contributed a lot in this. He used to serve as the executive producer."

Ketan Desai tells about the beginning of the relationship between his father and the Hinduja brothers, "My father Manmohan Desai made dozens of blockbuster super-duper hits from 1957 (Janam Janam Ke Phere) to 1993 (Anmol), but by the1980s, when he was planning to make a multi-star film 'Naseeb,' he suddenly landed into financial trouble. He was honest in terms of money and always used to calculate everything on time. Along with three superstars and three heroines of the time, hundreds of actors were to be cast for various parts in 'Naseeb'. Amitabh Bachchan, Shatrughan Sinha, Rishi Kapoor, Hema Malini, Reena Rai, Kim, and many more actors were to work. At that time, he hardly had any money, and he was looking for a partner on the formula of 50-50. One day our lawyer, Mr. M. L. Ranjit, told my father about the Hinduja brothers and advised him to meet them. The formula of 50-50 was that writing, directing, producing and all the work would be done by my father, and some other person would invest the money. Whether it is profit or loss, both would divide it among themselves. Father was also ready to pay interest on that money as well. He met Srichand Hinduja and Ashok Hinduja. He signed an agreement with the Hinduja brothers. It was the nobility of the Hinduja brothers that they said that they would not charge interest on the capital and the profits would be split in half, but if there was a loss, it would not be divided, and the Hinduja brothers would bear the entire loss. 'Naseeb' became a super hit. The film did good business in all regions of India as well as abroad."

"The manner of functioning of the Hinduja brothers was amazing. Once they believed in someone, they would not ask for anything else. They had placed a bet of about 4 to 5 crore at that time by trusting my father (Manmohan Desai). The shooting for 'Naseeb' was done in several parts. Father repeatedly invited Ashok Hinduja to watch the film's rushes, but he always maintained that he would watch the entire film once it was ready. Whenever the shooting was to take place, I used to make a budget and give it to Khushal Chhabria who would pass it on to Ashok Hinduja, and then Ashok Hinduja would issue the cheque immediately. They never delayed the payments. If they wanted, they could have kept the money for a month and earned interest on it. The Hinduja brothers knew very well how to do business. It was not the money but the intention that mattered."

"Naseeb was made at that time for about 4.5 crore rupees, which is equivalent to 250 crore today. Ashok Hinduja knew that the maximum amount of 75 lakh rupees was given to Amitabh Bachchan. When the Hinduja brothers refused to charge interest, my father said that he would then not charge any fee as the director of the film. That's why we shared a great equation with them. We had the blessings of Srichand Hinduja and got the support of Ashok Hinduja. Prakash Hinduja and Gopichand Hinduja used to play a big role in overseas distribution. We did many projects together later on. People used to call my father as Reserve Bank of India of the film industry. In those days, producers used to give lab letters to the film artists, which meant that the film would not go from the lab till the artists did not receive their full money, and only then they used to return that letter to the lab. Actually, in those days the artists used to get the money in several installments in which advance (signing amount), lab letter, and dubbing delivery were the main ones. But my father used to keep his accounts so accurate that he never gave lab letters to anyone. He always paid money to everyone on time. He used to start shooting for the film only when the money was in his hands. And everyone knew that their money was safe with him. He had a very clean image. The same thing was said about the Hinduja brothers. That's why we enjoyed such a long and healthy association".

"The matchless pair of Manmohan Desai and Amitabh Bachchan was called 'Maghi Bida Paan' by many, in which two 'bida paans' are connected by a skewer. Father had promised Amitabh Bachchan that he would not make any film without him. Whenever my father invited him to narrate his script, he would refuse. He had full faith in my father. When my father announced the film 'Coolie' without even signing Amitabh Bachchan, people asked Amitabh Bachchan if he was worried? He replied that if the announcement hadn't been made then he would have been worried. Now the tension was over. The pairing of my father (Manmohan Desai) and Amitabh Bachchan was amazing. He had full faith in Amitabh Bachchan so much so that Amitabh would nail the part exactly the way he had written for him. Once he even told Amitabh Bachchan, "The difference between you and me is that you ask if you would be able to do justice to a role and I know for sure that you can."

When we were making the film 'Mard' (1985) with the Hinduja brothers, Amitabh Bachchan was suddenly diagnosed with a disease that afflicts only one in ten crores (100 million) people. The danger was great as he had suffered a near-fatal injury during the shooting of the film 'Coolie' just two years before and had miraculously survived. This disease is called myasthenia gravis, in which the muscles of the body stop working and the person becomes paralyzed. He asked my father to take some other actor instead. Father declined, saying that he had changed the script and made his role like James Bond in a wheelchair with a sten gun. But fortunately, Amitabh recovered soon due to everyone's prayers. His mother Teji Bachchan recited Hanuman Chalisa , day and night, praying for his recovery and her prayers were answered.

Overseas, the films of my father and the Hinduja brothers with Amitabh Bachchan met with tremendous success. Advance booking of up to four weeks used to be quite normal. Our film 'Amar Akbar Anthony' met with immense success all over the world. The reason for this was that it propagated a message of national unity. The audience yearned for films of Manmohan Desai and Amitabh Bachchan, eagerly waiting for them. Ticket sellers who used to sell tickets in black outside the cinema halls in Mumbai too used to wait for their films to release. Once a man who married his three daughters after selling our movie tickets in black came to our office and requested my father to come with him to his home for five minutes. When father came to know about the real story, he was greatly surprised. When he went to that man's house, he saw that the man had called his three daughters and their husbands. They were all waiting for my father. The man asked her daughters and their husbands to seek blessings by touching the feet of my father because he felt it was because of my father only he could get his daughters married. He himself touched my father's feet. That black marketeer told his daughters, "Manmohan Desai is your real father because I could get you married only by selling tickets for his films in black."

In Beirut,my film 'Chandi Sona' ran Housefull for 50 weeks: Sanjay Khan

The film actor, director, and producer Sanjay Khan has known the Hinduja brothers since the days when the Hinduja family lived in the Khar area of Mumbai. Raj Kapoor used to come there. Sanjay Khan says, "My friendship with Raj Kapoor and the Hinduja brothers started from there. In those days they were in dry fruit business. Srichand is a man of exquisite taste. My friendship with Gopichand, Prakash, and Ashok grew deep during that period. There after I used to travel to Tehran and later to London as well. We had a friend in London named Nirmal Sethia. Srichand and I used to go to his place a lot and we would do a lot of partying there. We have spent so many evenings with Raj Kapoor in their Khar house in Mumbai. That's where I planned the film 'Abdullah' (1980) with Raj Kapoor.

Sanjay Jumani, Sanjay Khan, and Ashok Hinduja

"The Hinduja brothers released my film 'Chandi Sona' (1977) overseas. I was surprised that this film gave a tremendous competition to Francis Ford Coppola's 'Godfather' at the box office in Beirut (Lebanon) and ran housefull for 50 weeks. The movie also did well in London. It ran housefull wherever it was screened by the Hinduja brothers across the globe. Parveen Babi, Prem Nath, Danny, Iftikhar, Kamini Kaushal, Asrani, Ranjeet and I starred in the movie. The story of the film was also very interesting and it kept the viewers on the edge of their seats till

QURBANI

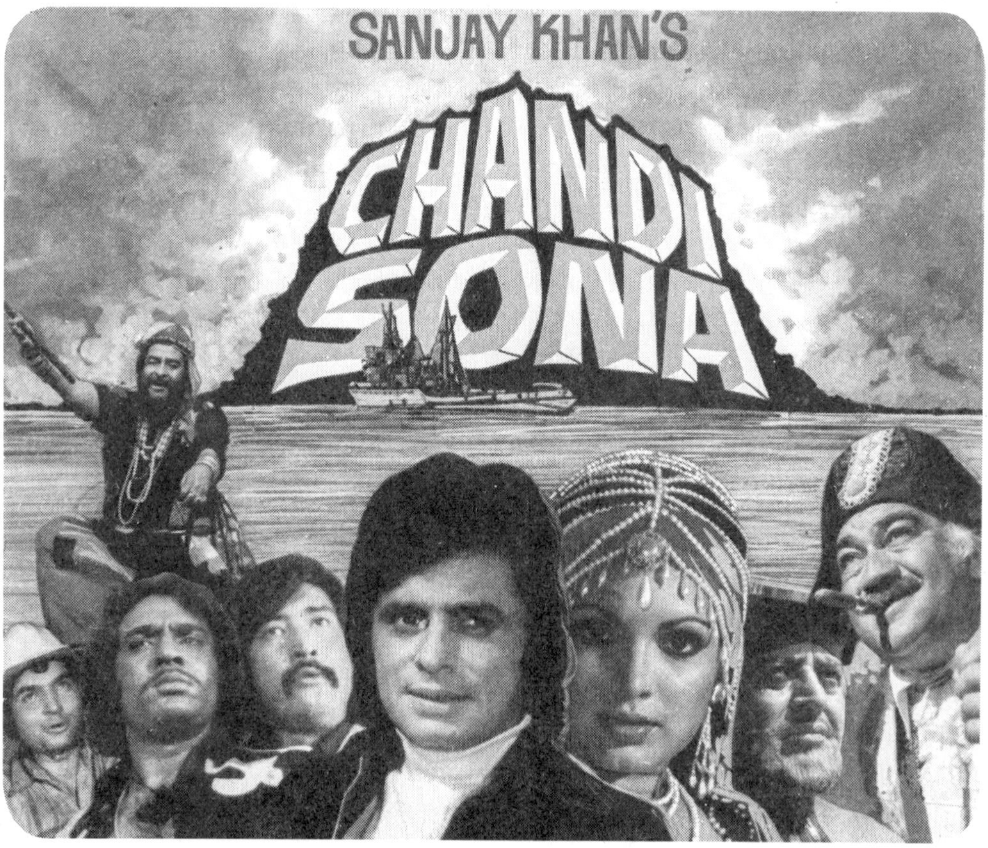
SANJAY KHAN'S
CHANDI SONA

the end. Raj Kapoor also played a small role in it. This was the first film that was shot in Mauritius. We had become good friends with Prime Minister Chacha Ram Ghoolam (Sivasagar Ramgoolam Kushwaha, 18-09-1900--15-12-1985). He used to come to see our film shoots also."

"It is also a strange coincidence that I made three films—'Chandi Sona,' 'Abdullah,' and 'Kala Dhandha Gore Log' (1986)—but collaborated with the Hinduja brothers on only one of them. Still, we remained close friends. Raj Kapoor was a common friend of ours. When I offered him a role in 'Abdullah' and asked him how much money he would charge, he laughed and said with outstretched arms—'This much.' One evening we went to a wedding together. There I gave him one lakh rupees in cash. He refused and said that if Shashi (Kapoor) would make a film then would I charge a fee from him? But I too was adamant and said that it was the promise of a Pathan and that he would have to accept the money."

"People in those days were mostly like that. At first I got small roles in Chetan Anand's 'Haqeeqat' and Rajshri Production's Satyen Bose-directed 'Dosti'. Both the films came in 1964. But even though my roles were small, my work was well received by the audience and film critics. Since then, I have done a lot of films and later made several television serials like 'The Sword of Tipu Sultan' from 1989-90. During this time, I saw that the Hinduja brothers continued to do good things for our film industry. I share a relationship with them that cannot be seen from a business point of view,"

The Hinduja Brothers had a close Relationship with Dev Anand and his Company Navketan since the Beginning: Amit Khanna

Writer-director Amit Khanna, who had been Indian films' evergreen actor Dev Anand's assistant in Navketan Films, recalls his meetings with the Hinduja brothers, saying, "Although, Indian films have been shown abroad since 1935, the Hinduja brothers have made a mark in the overseas market. These people previously lived in the Khar area of Mumbai and their office was on Charni Road. There is also a street in Khar called 'Parmanand Deepchand Hinduja Marg,' which is named after their father. At that time there were mainly three distributors of Overseas – Harbans Lal, Magan Bhai Sabani, and Parmanand, father of filmmaker Gul Anand (Khatta Meetha)".

Amit Khanna

"I remember that they screened Dev Anand's first two films, 'Guide' (1965) and 'Jewel Thief' (1967), and later 'Hare Rama Hare Krishna' (1971) and 'Swami Dada' (1982) abroad. I remember that films of Raj Kapoor, Dilip Kumar, and Dev Anand used to do the most business overseas. The Hinduja brothers also invested money in some of Dev Sahab's films. When 'Guide' was specially screened at the Cannes Film Festival, the Hinduja brothers organized a party in his honor at their house. Actually, they have been organizing a party at their house there every year during the Cannes Film Festival for the promotion of Indian films. Dev Anand also used to go there.

"I had the chance to visit their house in London with Dev Saheb three or four times. The Hinduja brothers take great care of their guests, although the food is

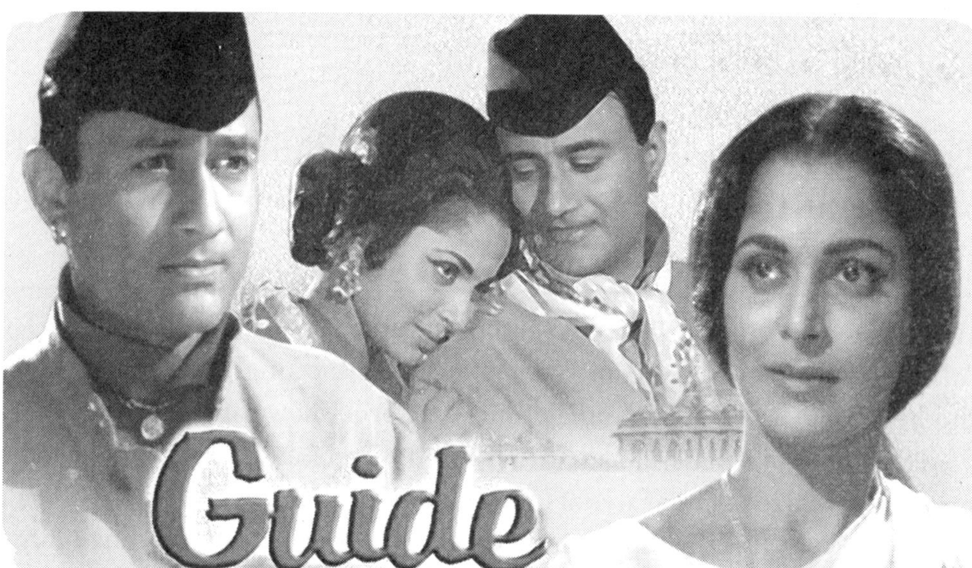

always vegetarian. The Hinduja brothers had a very close relationship with Dev Anand and his company Navketan Films, right from the very beginning. Although Isar Das Naumal used to invest money in Navketan's initial films, later the Hinduja brothers started investing. On the other hand, India Today Group Chairman Aroon Purie's father Vidya Vilas Purie had invested money in the initial films of Raj Kapoor and B.R. Chopra. When the Hinduja family came into the cinema business, at that time no big industrialist wanted to get associated with it because cinema then was considered a small business and it took a lot of time and effort. It's really commendable that even in those days (1955-1978), the Hinduja brothers used to take Raj Kapoor and other Indian artists to Iran by chartered planes. The Hinduja brothers have made an important contribution to the history of Indian cinema, which people are forgetting today."

Prakash Hinduja Introduced me to Jill Jacob, the President of the Cannes Film Festival: S.M. Khan

S. M. Khan

S.M. Khan, former Director-General (September 2008 – February 2011), Directorate of Film Festivals, Ministry of Information and Broadcasting, Government of India, recalls, "Prakash Hinduja was a frequent visitor to the Indian Pavilion during the Cannes Film Festival. That's how I met him. He used to come himself and often brought with him some of the influential people associated with cinema who could help in promoting Indian films internationally. He used to participate in every activity of the Indian Pavilion. He always said that he was ready to do everything that would elevate India's stature in the field of cinema at the international level. Prakash Hinduja also got me and the Indian delegation to meet Jill Jacob, President of the Cannes Film Festival in 2009-10, with the aim of exploring avenues for developing a market for Indian films in France as well as increasing the activities of exchange between India and France in the field of cinema. All these efforts resulted in the signing of a co-production agreement between India and France."

"The Hinduja brothers' dinner at the Cannes Film Festival often used to be a topic of discussion. They hosted a lavish dinner for the promotion of Indian films at the Le Grand Hotel in Cannes on the evening of 14 May, 2010, wherein they invited film personalities from around the world who were attending the Cannes Film Festival. Indian guests included me and the Indian delegation along with a large number of Indian film stars including

Amitabh Bachchan, Aishwarya Rai, Subhash Ghai, Prasoon Joshi, Rakesh Roshan, Hrithik Roshan, and Manisha Koirala. In those days, Ashok Hinduja's daughter Ambika Hinduja's film 'Teen Patti' (director Leena Yadav) was launched there in which Ben Kingsley of Richard Attenborough's 'Gandhi' (1982) fame and Amitabh Bachchan played the lead roles."

Jill Jacob: The man who made Cannes Film Festival the most important film festival in the world

"Prakash Hinduja still keeps giving me many constructive suggestions. He suggests that a great film should be made on the historic meeting between Romain Rolland and Mahatma Gandhi which should be shown at film festivals around the world. Mahatma Gandhi stayed for five days in December 1931 at the Villa Leonette, the home of the great French scholar Romain Rolland, a Nobel laureate in Switzerland, near the French border. On 14 September 2019, on the 150th birth anniversary of Mahatma Gandhi, the President of India, Ram Nath Kovind, went there and unveiled the statue of Mahatma Gandhi. In the same ceremony, the intersection was named after Mahatma Gandhi in memory of that historic visit. Unfortunately, I am no longer in the government and the times have changed."

Pleased with my tunes, Ashok Hinduja Fed Me Gajar Ka Halwa: Anu Malik

Anu Malik (Anwar Sardar Malik), who once ruled Hindi film music, recalls his early days of struggle, saying that he would not have achieved such quick success if Manmohan Desai had not made him meet Ashok Hinduja. It was forty years ago when Ashok Hinduja and Manmohan Desai were

making the film 'Mard' (1985) with the then superstar Amitabh Bachchan. In those days, Hindi film music was dominated by composers like Laxmikant Pyarelal, Kalyanji Anandji, Rahul Dev Burman. Laxmikant Pyarelal used to be Manmohan Desai's favourite musician. Anu Malik says, "I was around 20-22 years old then and I hadn't tasted much success by then. One day, I dared to make Manmohan Desai listen to some of my tunes. Manmohan Desai was at the top of the film industry in those days and a film directed by him was guaranteed to be a super hit at the box office. He took me to the Hinduja Brother's Mumbai home saying that if Ashok Hinduja liked my tunes, he would take me as a music composer in his film 'Mard'. I took my musical instruments and followed him to the Hinduja Bungalow in Juhu. I played some tunes that I had prepared for 'Mard' there. One of the songs had the opening lines—"Main Hoon Mard Tangewala, Mujhe Dushman Kya Marega, Mera Dost Hai Uparwala." The second song was—"Sun Rubiya, Tujhse Pyar Ho Gaya, Main Tera Tangewala, Tu Meri Tangewali." For the film, I had composed a 'Mata Ka Bhajan' with three alternate tunes for it. I played all three tunes to Ashok Hinduja. His musical sense was amazing. He chose the same tune that Manmohan Desai had already liked. The Bhajan was—"O Maa Sheronwaali, Maa Meri Maa Se Mila De Mujhe." Ashok Hinduja liked all my tunes, and I got the job. So pleased he was with my tunes, he fed me homemade Gajar Ka Halwa (a traditional carrot and milk-based sweet preparation) from his kitchen. I can never forget that evening. Just imagine, the way he gave a 20-22 old like me the opportunity to compose music for a big-budget Amitabh Bachchan film, it was nothing short of a miracle for me. Since then, I have remained friends with him."

"I wonder why there is no talk of the Hinduja brothers despite making such a huge contribution to the development of Hindi cinema. The truth is that the Hinduja brothers have laid the foundation of Bollywood and helped everyone. Coincidentally, every film in which they invested money went on to become a super hit. The corporate culture we talk about in cinema today started with the Hinduja brothers' company 'Aasia Films'. The first big film of my life was 'Mard' in which 'Aasia Films' had invested money. Hindujas are not just big people, they are also loving people. There will be others who invest money in cinema, but Ashok Hinduja had vision for the Indian Cinema. This is the understanding that made him successful. It used to happen in those days that as soon as the Hindujas agreed to invest money in a film, it used to be a guarantee that the film will get made. The director used to discover a new self-confidence. For us artists, the Hinduja brothers are the ones with the hearts of the kings. Whenever something new happens in the world, the Hinduja brothers call artists and intellectuals together to host a discussion around it."

Hinduja Brothers Never Sued Anyone in Court for Money: Subhash Sharma

Subhash Sharma

Subhash Sharma, the distributor of the superhit, multi-starrer film of its time, 'Suhaag' (1979, Manmohan Desai), says, "The Hinduja brothers helped hundreds of filmmakers with their money. These people were honest in business. They bought the film 'Suhaag' from me and screened it in the UK, US, Singapore, and various other countries. The film made a tenfold profit. These people never used to approach anyone. If anyone who had to do business, he used to go to them. They used to make agreements in advance, but these people never sued anyone in the court for money and did not punish anyone. The Hindujas would simply pardon the person, if he could not pay back the money. In that era, the film 'Suhaag' was made for Rs. 2.25 crore. Just imagine the Hinduja brothers did publicity of 550 films in 1964."

10

Epilogue

How this book came to be written has been discussed in detail in the first chapter. In the end, all I can say is that the Hinduja brothers should have continued their cinema business in some form or the other for a few more years. They should have documented their endeavors of taking Indian cinema around the world, which would have inspired many coming generations. I suggest that a museum should be built in Mumbai which depicts this golden history of cinema. Today's young generation who loves cinema should at least know how that period was, and how Indian cinema got recognition across the world due to the efforts of the Hinduja brothers. All in all, it was a cultural, social campaign to take Indian culture around the world through cinema, which should have continued in some form or the other. One thing I will always regret is why I didn't meet the Hinduja brothers ten years ago when I went to attend the Cannes Film Festival for the first time in 2013. Many people associated with this history were alive then and their experiences could have been included in this book.

The one thing that inspired me to write this book is why nothing was ever spoken about the people who laid the foundation of Bollywood sixty five to seventy years ago. In this regard, I met hundreds of people from the film and business world, all of whom were surprised to hear from me.

There are many unheard stories in this book. It is in a way an attempt to revive the forgotten history. Today Iranian cinema is known all over the world, but the history of the success of Hindi cinema in the same country Iran is almost forgotten. When I went to Tehran in September 2012 at the invitation of the Iranian president, Mahmoud Ahmadinejad, and tried to talk to people about Hindi cinema, I was surprised to find that no one even there now knows anything about this history. When this book will be published in Persian, it is possible that the young generation of Iran will get to know about this golden history. When I went to Egypt for the 42nd Cairo International Film Festival (2020), people knew very little about Hindi cinema there too. No one knows much about the government's cinema hall in Cairo where Raj Kapoor's film 'Sangam' ran house full for a year. That is why it is necessary to publish the Arabic edition of this book. Another difficulty I faced was that very few documents could be found while rediscovering this history. The main reason for this was that the Hinduja brothers never made any effort to take credit for their contribution, nor did they show any interest in it. Generally, the Hinduja family kept a distance from the media, so there is hardly any information about them in the magazines published in the fifties and sixties. They also stayed away from film parties. Perhaps, one of the reasons for this may have been the promise made to their father Parmanand Deepchand Hinduja. However, a big task has been successfully completed.

Veteran actor of his time Manoj Kumar repeatedly expressed his desire to share his experiences. He was unable to do so because of his ill health. Amitabh Bachchan also had to write something and I had spoken to Karan Johar many times. Ramesh Sippy, Waheeda Rehman, Dev Anand's son Sunil Anand, Dilip Kumar's wife Saira Banu, Jackie Shroff, Anup Jalota, Randhir Kapoor, Subhash Ghai, Rakesh Bakshi, son of lyricist Anand Bakshi, Ranchhod Jumani, wife of Filmistan owner Tolaram Jalan Neena Jalan and many such people could not make themselves available for talks. Recentlyat the Rajasthan International Film Festival, Jodhpur, I met Sanjeev Goenka, associated with Filmistan Studios, who showed interest in this book. It is possible that in the second edition of this book, some more material may be included along with the discussions carried out with these people. In February 2020, Gopichand Hinduja suggested that onceI should also go to Iran once and do some more research for this book. Ashok Hinduja had also got all the arrangements made but some problems started in Iran and a few days later, due to COVID-19, a lockdown was imposed in India.

Today, if we talk about the quality, role, and market of Hindi cinema globally, the foundation to the scene that emerges was laid down by the Hinduja brothers in the fifties. They created a worldwide market for Hindi cinema in that era. It also came to the fore that when our film industry was going through a terrible recession, the Hinduja brothers rescued it. India got a huge amount of foreign capital due to their efforts. The government of India would have it on its records. Today, there is a huge market for Bollywood movies all over the world and our films are doing good business. All this was made possible because the Hinduja brothers built this market in the fifties. If today more efforts are made in this direction and Hindi films are screened again in these very countries where our films had registered commercial success, then this market can grow even bigger.

In the April 24th,1964 issue of 'Madhuri', the famous magazine of the Times of India Newspaper Group, a long but important interview of the famous French film critic Georges Sadoul by Vinod Krishna Tiwari has been published on pages 22-23, titled— 'Indian films in Europe.' In this interview, Georges Sadoul says at one point—"We want to see Indian civilization and culture in your films, not an imitation of the West."

This is the basic mantra due to which all the Indian films exported abroad by the Hinduja brothers were successful. An analysis of the cultural identity and the Indianness of those films can be very interesting in current times. What was it about those films that made the foreign audiences go crazy? Obviously, it was the Indian values shown in those films.

The phenomenal success of the films by producers and directors such as V Shantaram, Dev Anand, Raj Kapoor, Shakti Samanta, Rajshree Production, Manoj Kumar, Manmohan Desai, Ramanand Sagar, Mehboob Khan, GP Sippy, etc. abroad created a different history from 1954-1984.The global market for Hindi cinema that we see today was made possible because the Hinduja brothers had laid its foundation in 1954-55. The contribution of Raj Kapoor and his films in this is unmatched. The Indian films that are becoming successful overseas today are usually those films that we call parallel cinema, art cinema, or serious cinema. My conclusions are based on the world's most powerful film festivals like the Cannes, Berlin, Venice, Busan, Sundance, etc. which started with Vishnupant Govind Damle and Sheikh Fattelal's Marathi film 'Sant Tukaram' (1936) and Chetan Anand's 'Neecha Nagar' (1946) and later Satyajit Ray's film 'Pather Panchali' (1955) took this legacy forward. It is to be noted here that the Hinduja brothers focused on mainstream commercial cinema in Hindi rather than the marginal cinema, due to which our films today have such a huge market all over the world. I think all these subjects should at least be talked about. It is entirely due to their efforts that some position and respect also gets accorded to the mainstream cinema at the Cannes Film Festival, the world's biggest film festival.

Apart from Raj Kapoor's 'Sangam', Mehboob Khan's 'Mother India', and Ramanand Sagar's 'Aarzoo,' and 'Aankhen', it is pertinent to mention a few more films that set records of popularity and commercial success across the globe. Bimal Mitra's film 'Durgesh Nandini' (1956), based on the novel by Bankim Chandra Chattopadhyay, has been discussed, which was screened in Iran under the name 'Farman-e-Akbar'. Similarly, actor Dev Anand's film 'Guide' (1965) was released there in Persian under the name 'Rahnuma', directed by Vijay Anand. Rajshri Production's 'Dosti' and Rajesh Khanna starrer 'Hathi Mere Saathi' were also talked about a lot. V Shantaram's two films 'Do Aankhen Barah Haath' and 'Dr Kotnis Ki Amar Kahani' also did good business. The names of some more films can also be counted in this regard like Raj Kapoor's 'Aag', 'Shree 420', 'Awara', 'Jis Desh Mein Ganga Bahti Hai', 'Bobby', Prakash Arora's 'Boot Polish', Manoj Kumar's 'Upkar', 'Purab and Paschim', 'Roti, Kapda Aur Makan', 'Shor', 'Kranti', Pramod Chakraborty's 'Dream Girl', Ramesh Sippy's 'Sholay', Randhir Kapoor's 'Iman Dharam', Dev Anand's 'Baazi', 'Jewel Thief', 'Hare Rama Hare Krishna', Dilip Kumar's 'Ram Aur Shyam', Hema Malini's 'Sita Aur Geeta', Raj Kumar's 'Paigham' and 'Dil Ek Mandir', Shammi Kapoor's 'Brahmachari', Rajendra Kumar's 'Mere Mehboob', Yash Johar's 'Dostana,' and Amitabh Bachchan's all major movies, etc.

Now this book is dedicated to the readers. Whatever has been missed, we will try to include it in its future editions.